MANDALAS

COLORING BOOK FOR KIDS
FUN AND RELAXING

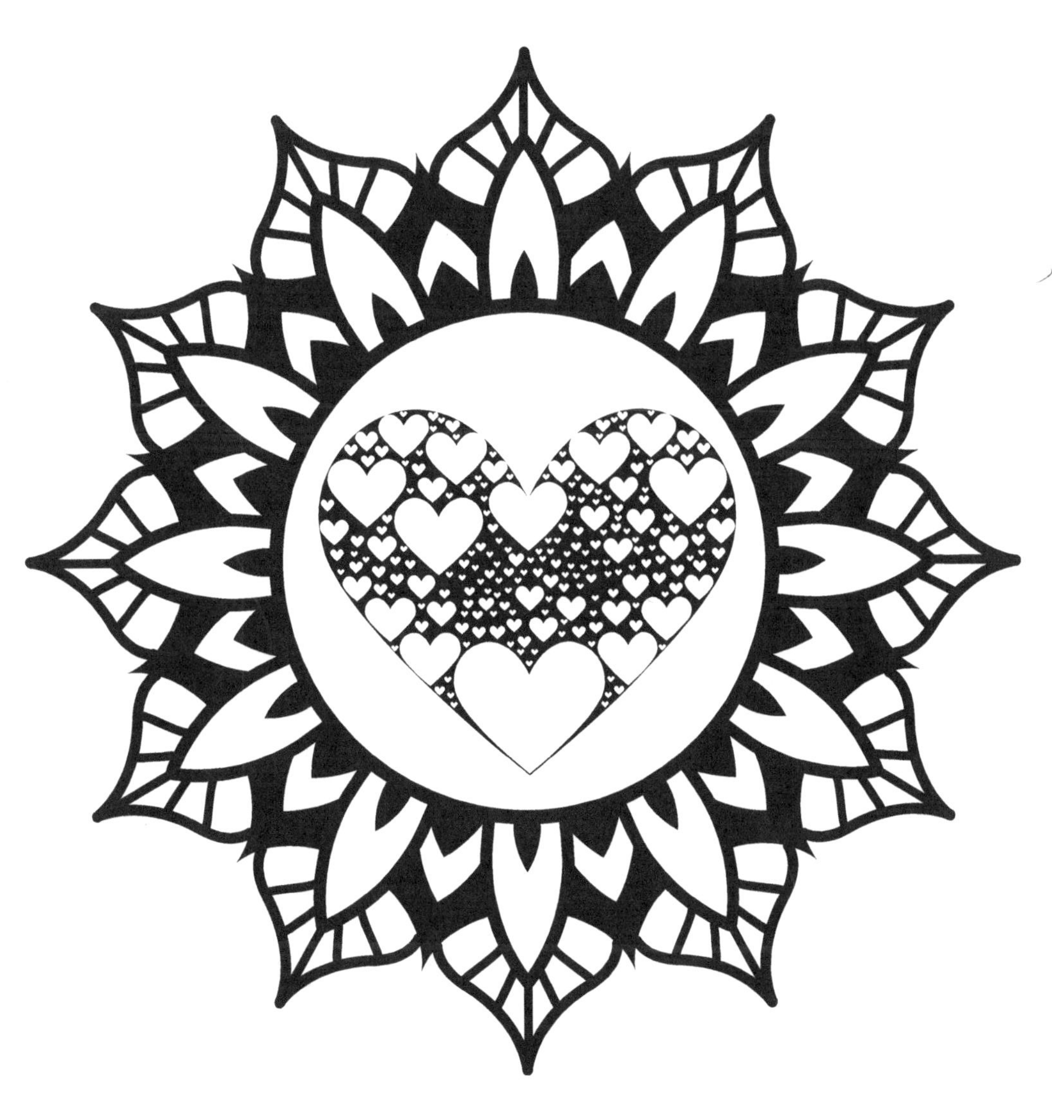

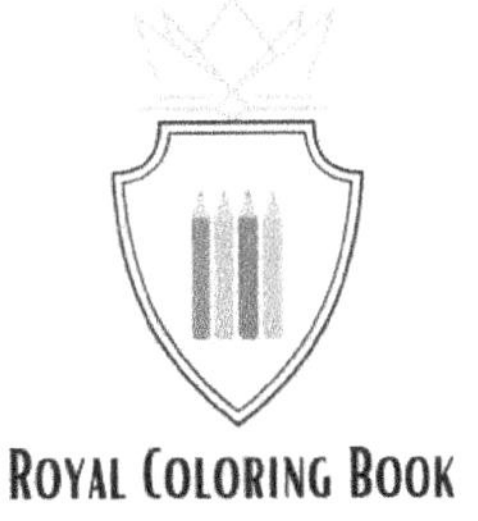

ROYAL COLORING BOOK

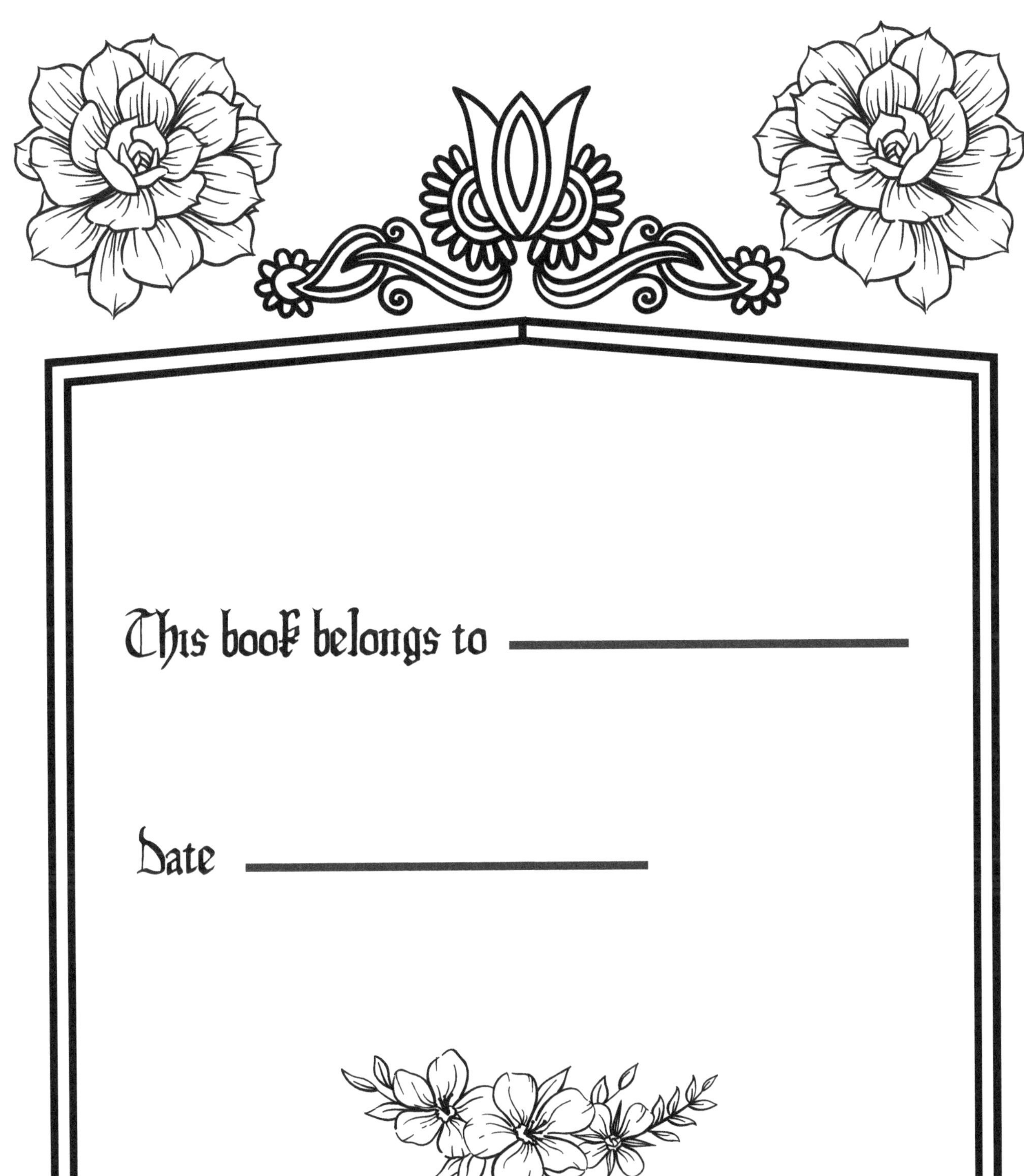

This book belongs to ___________________

Date ___________________

Color Test Page

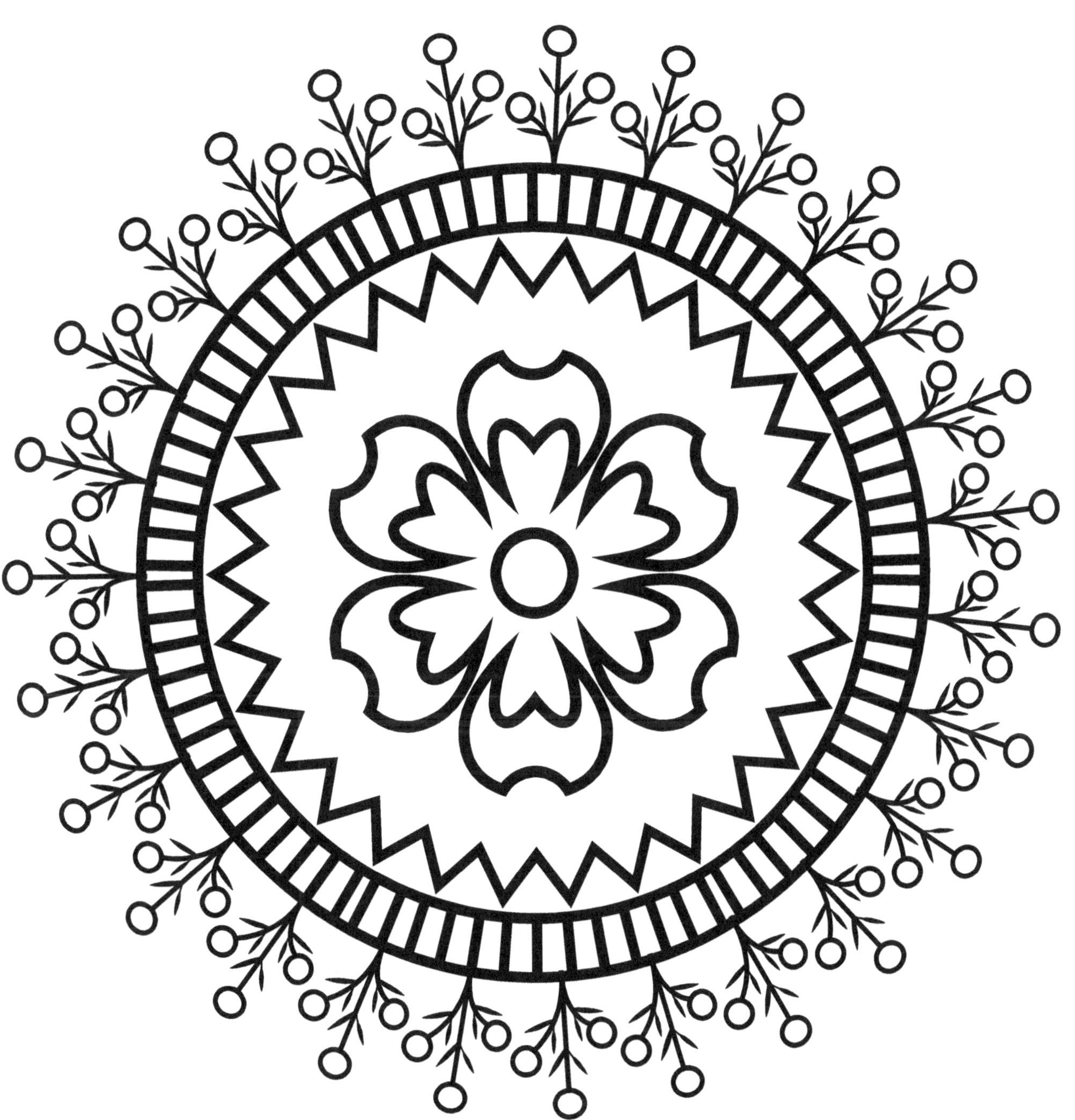

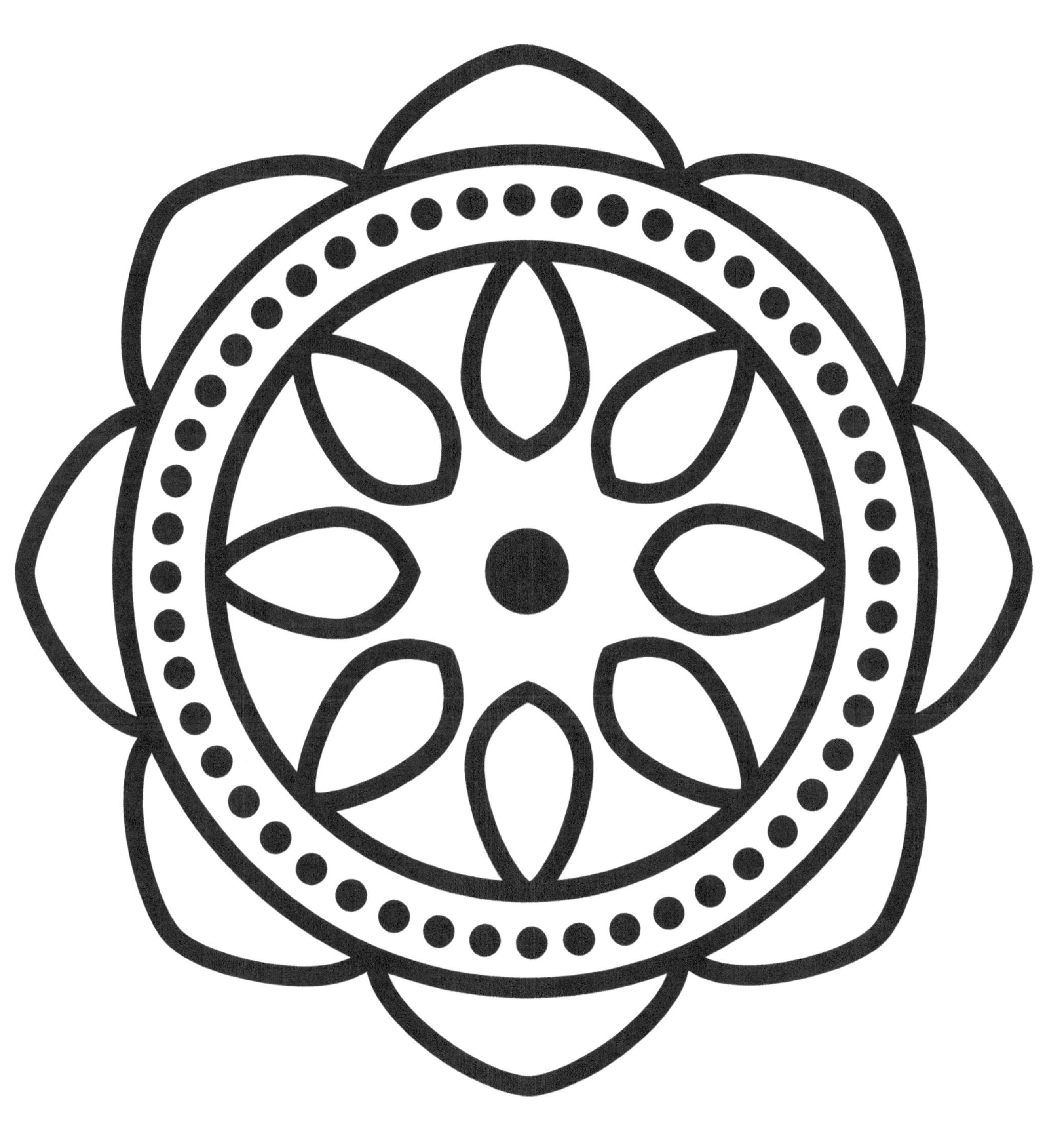

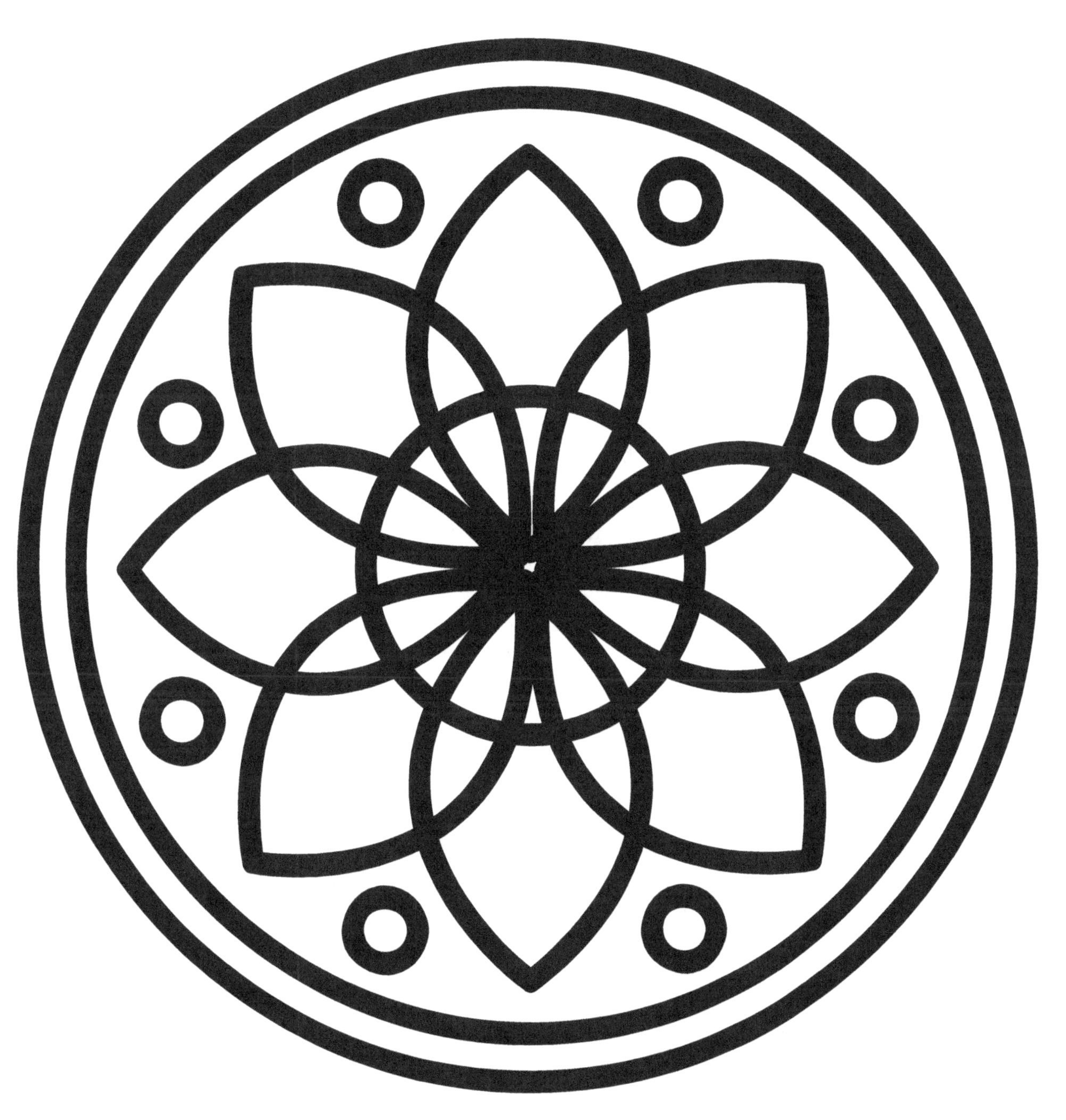

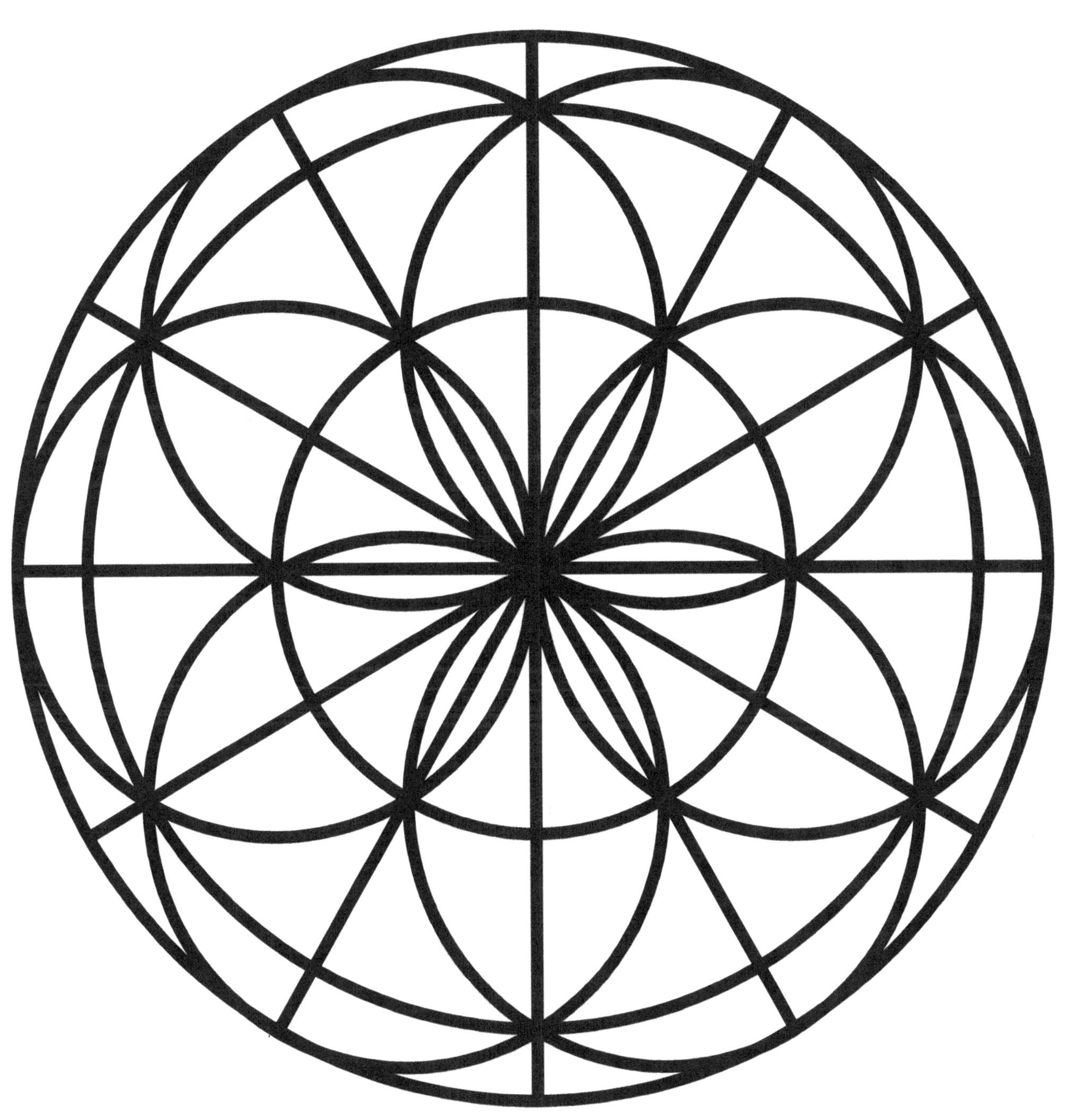

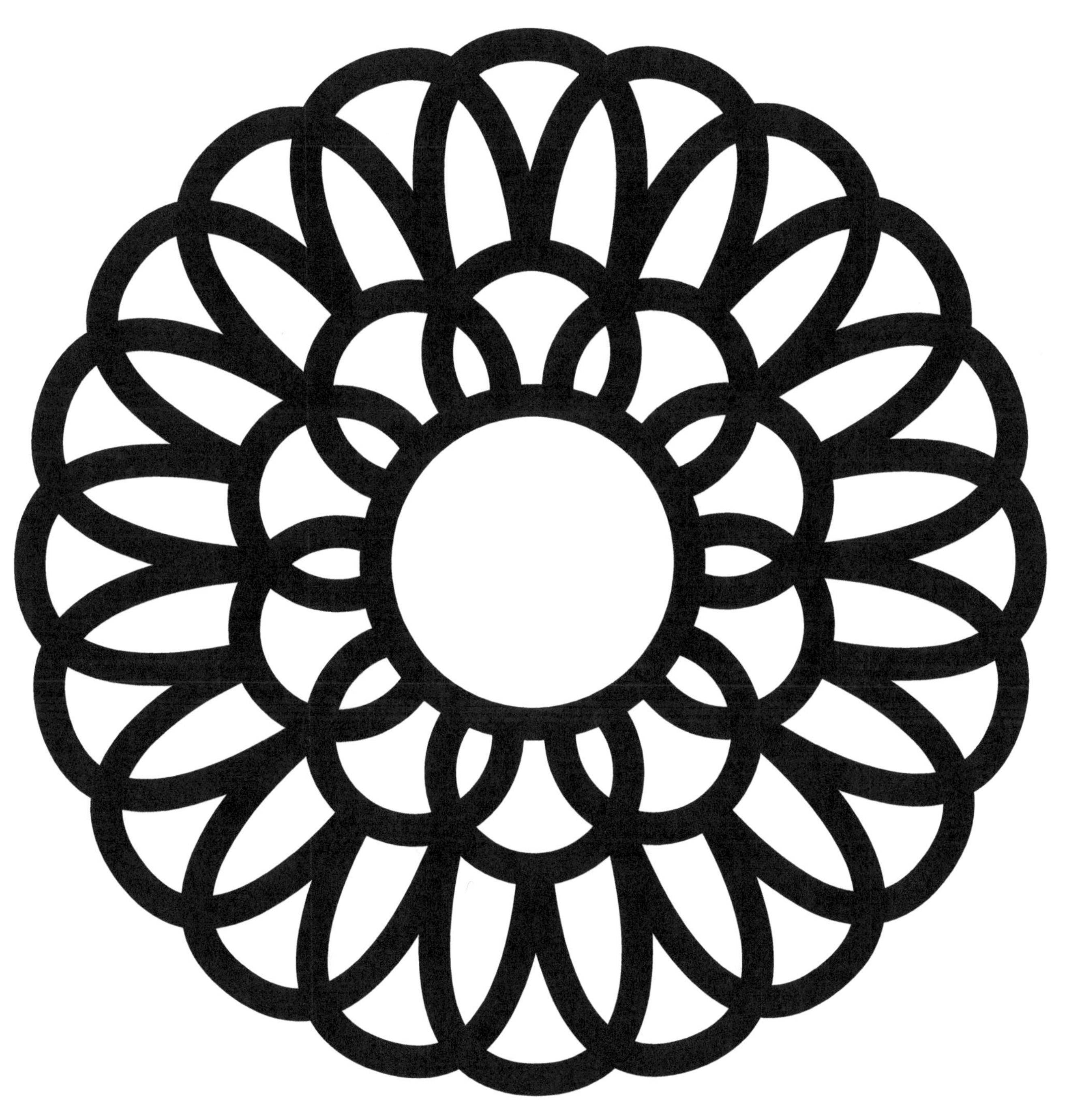

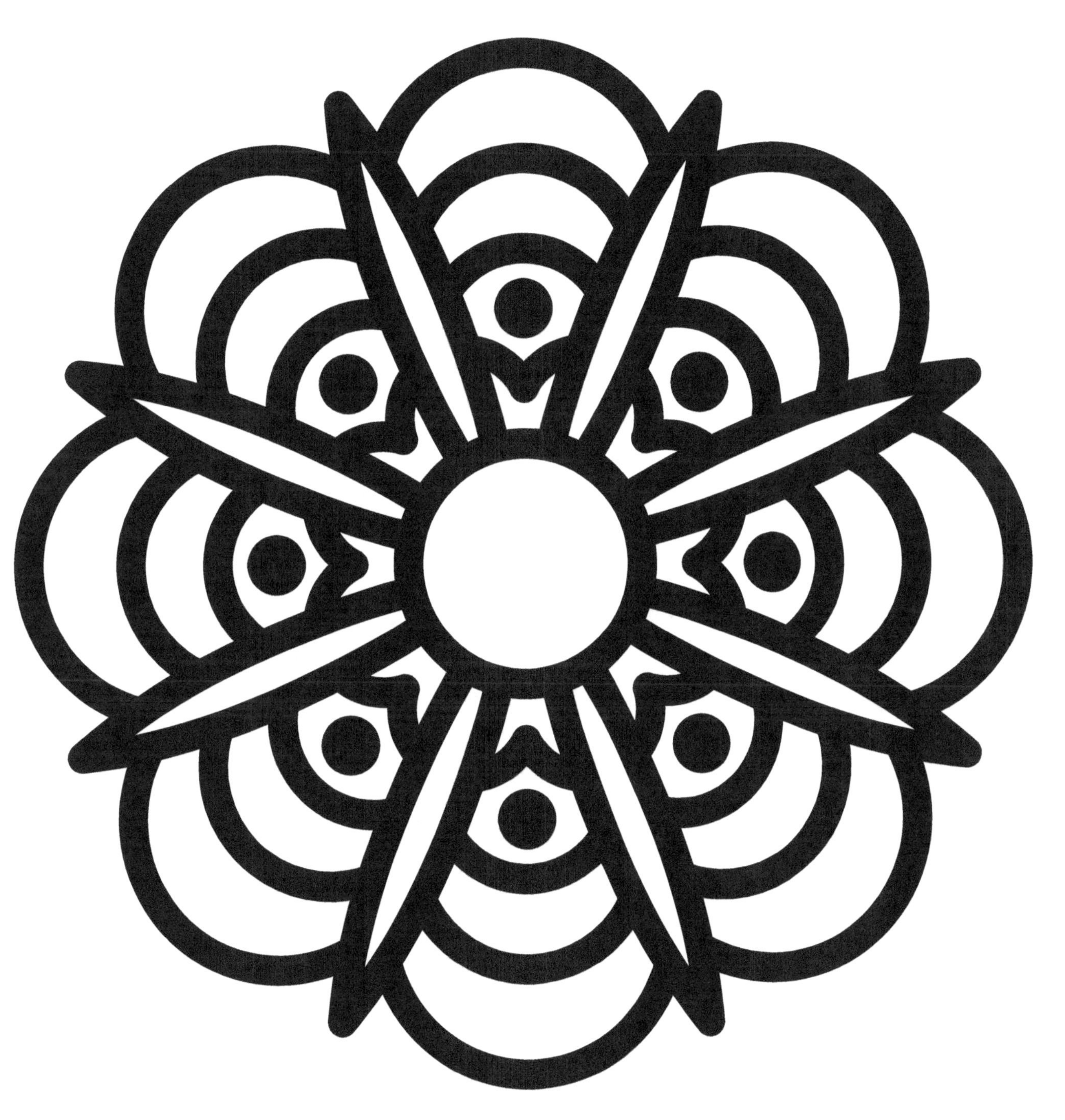

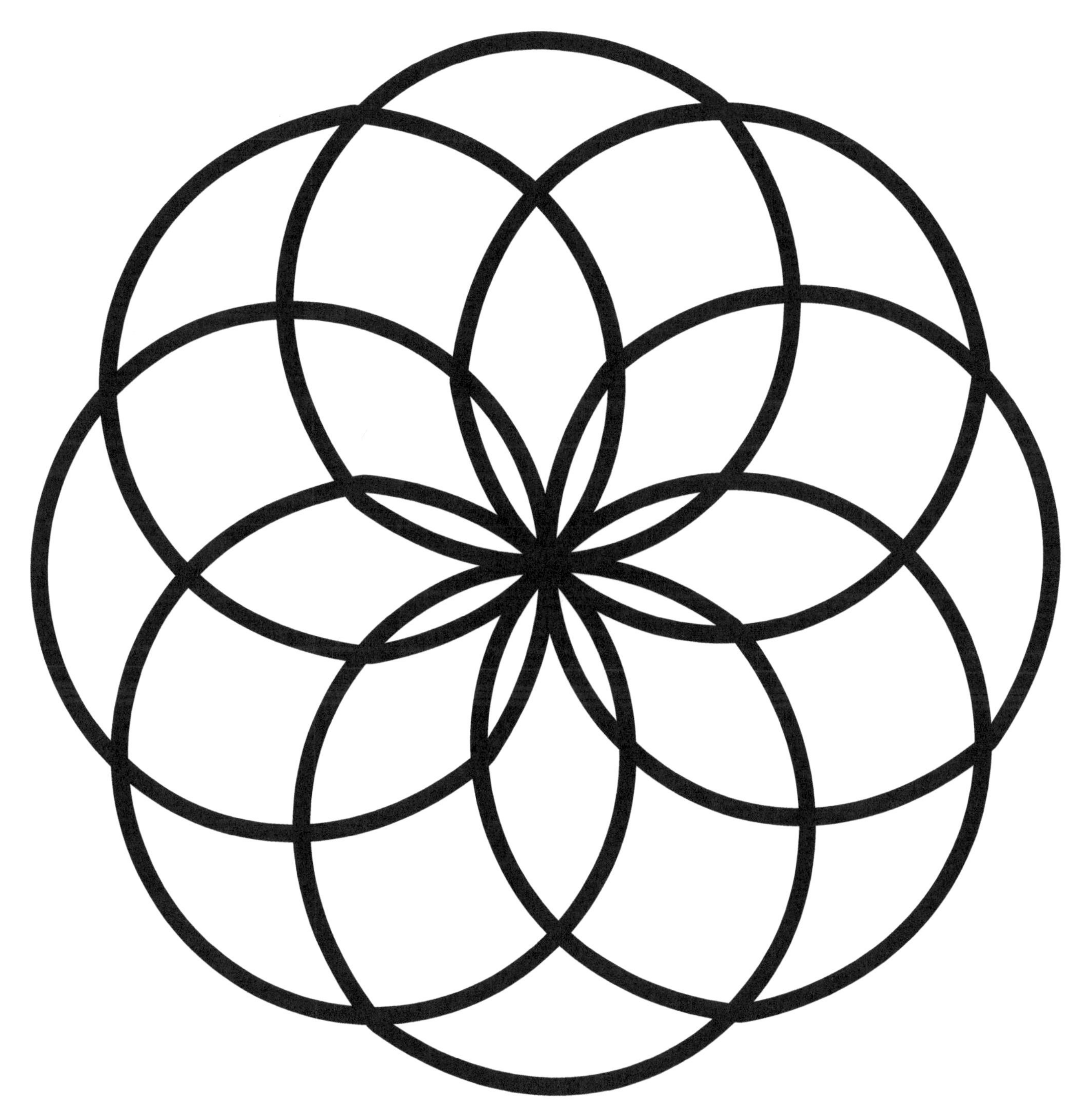

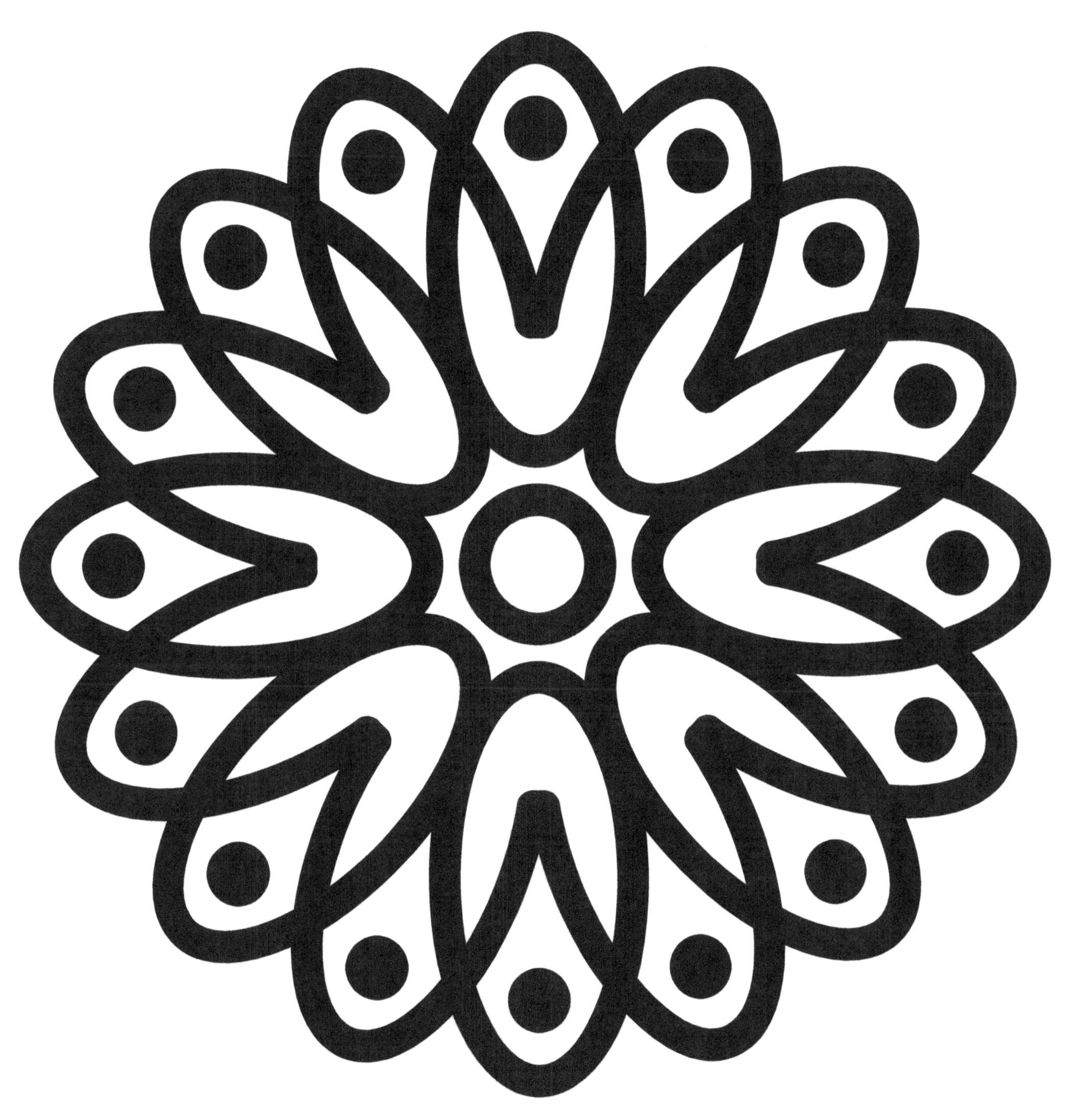

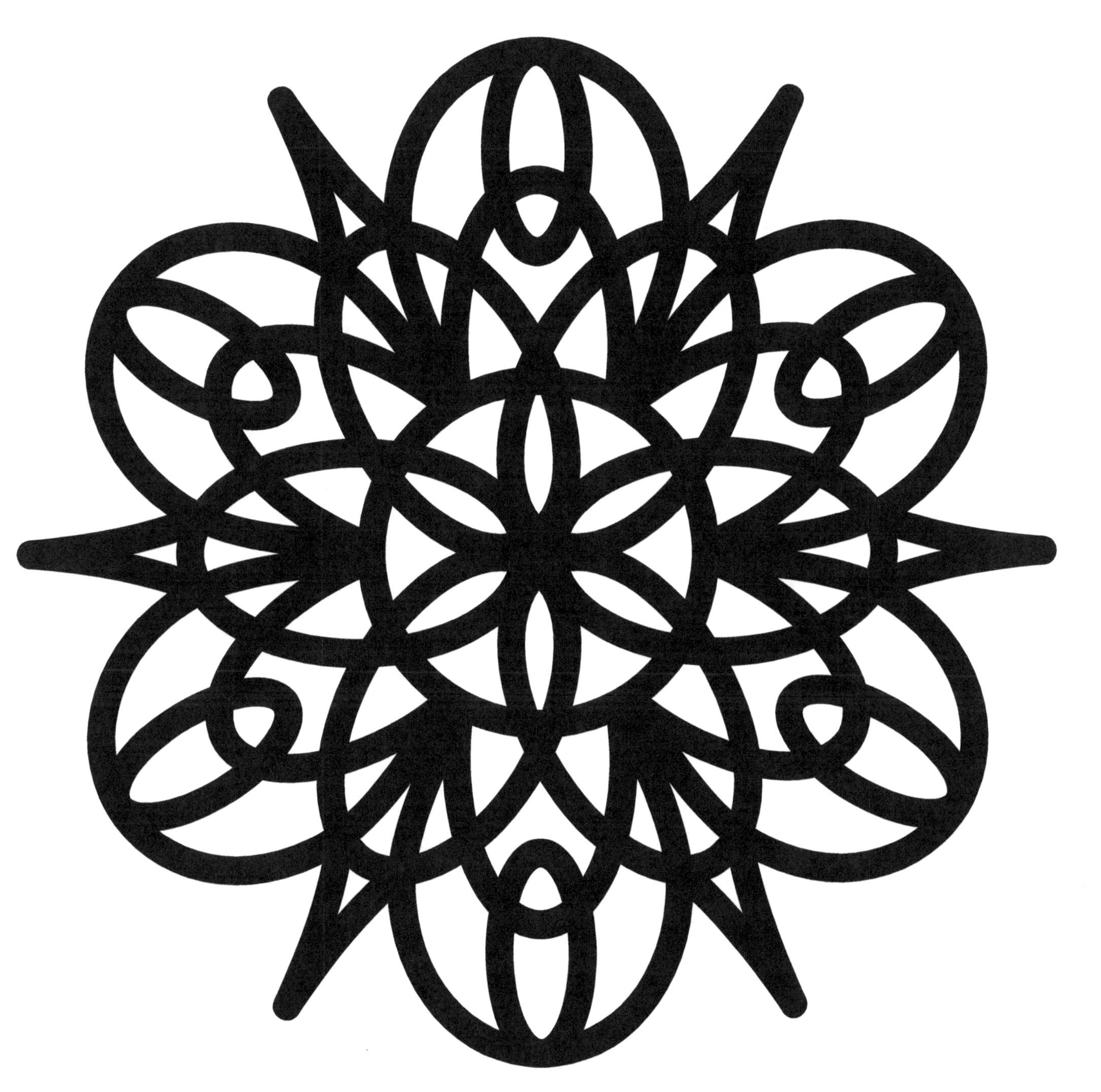

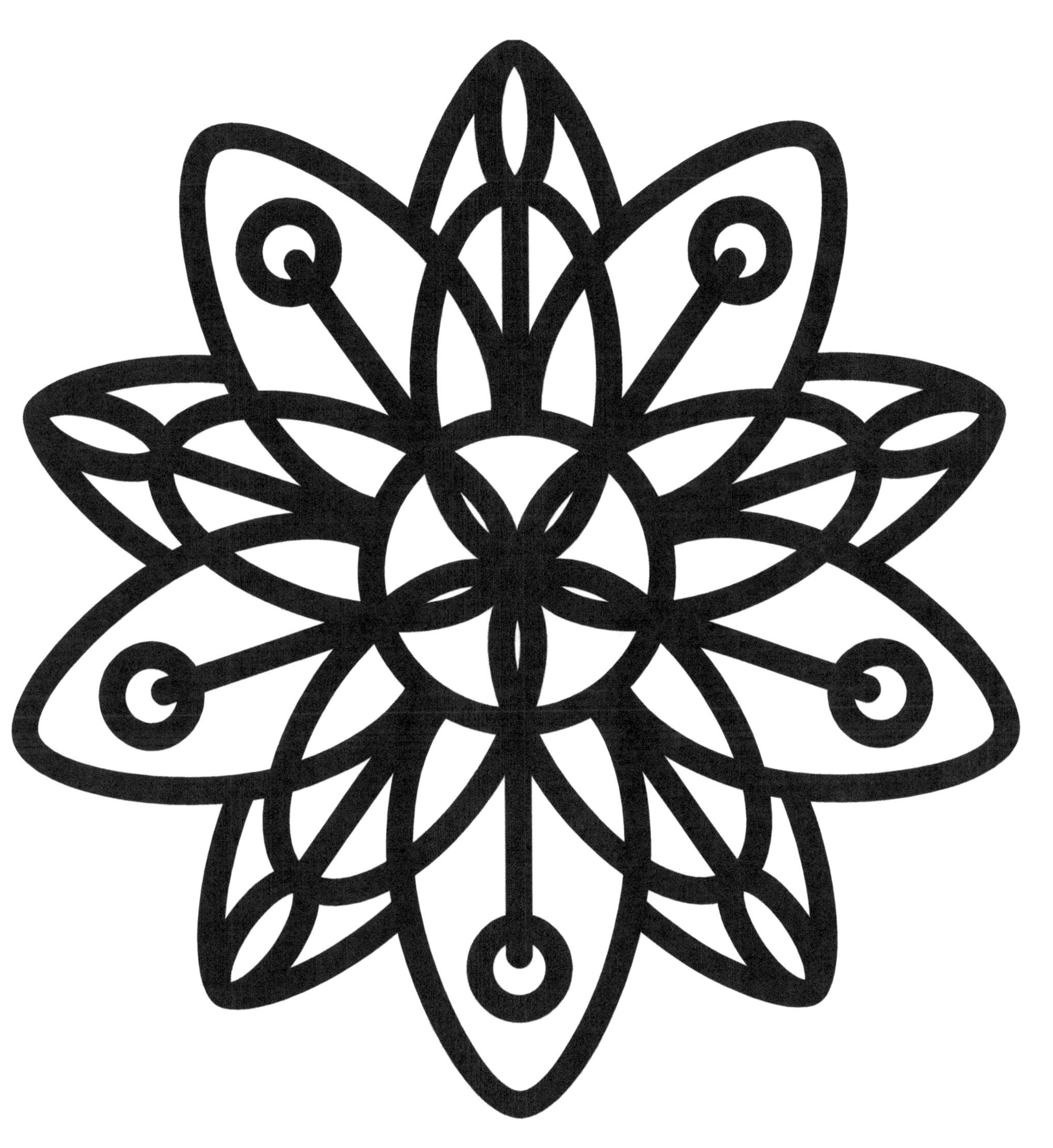

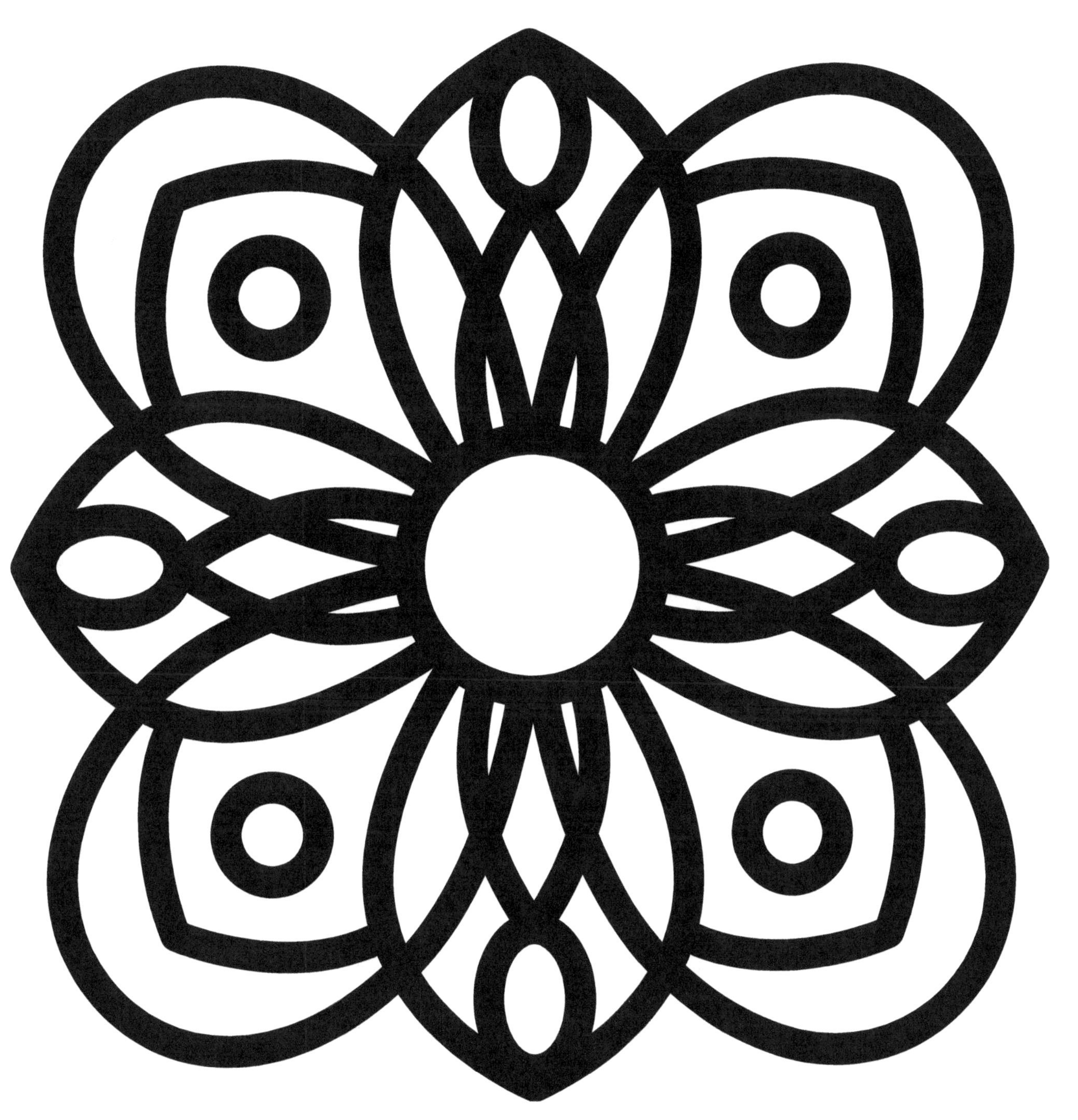

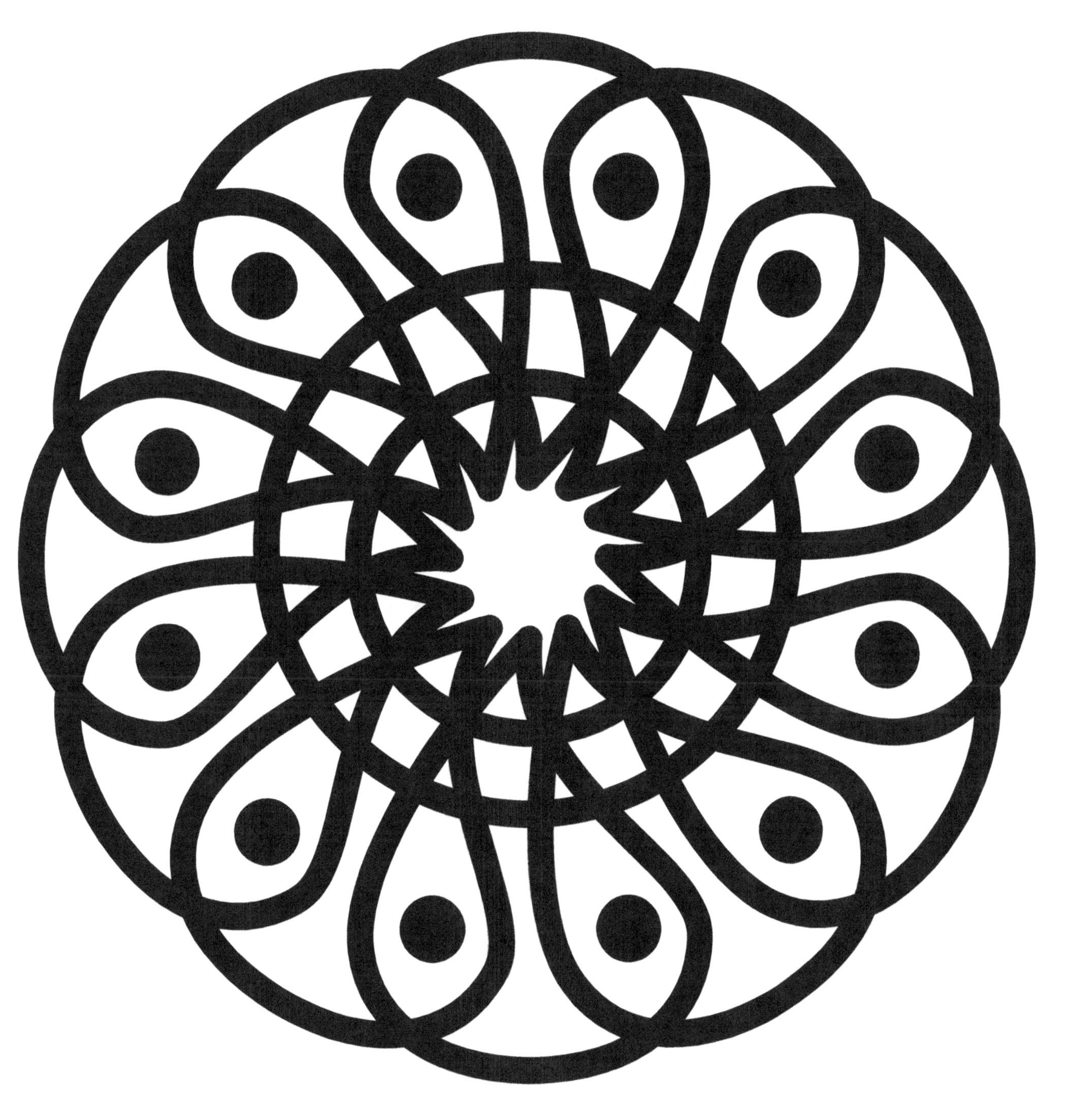

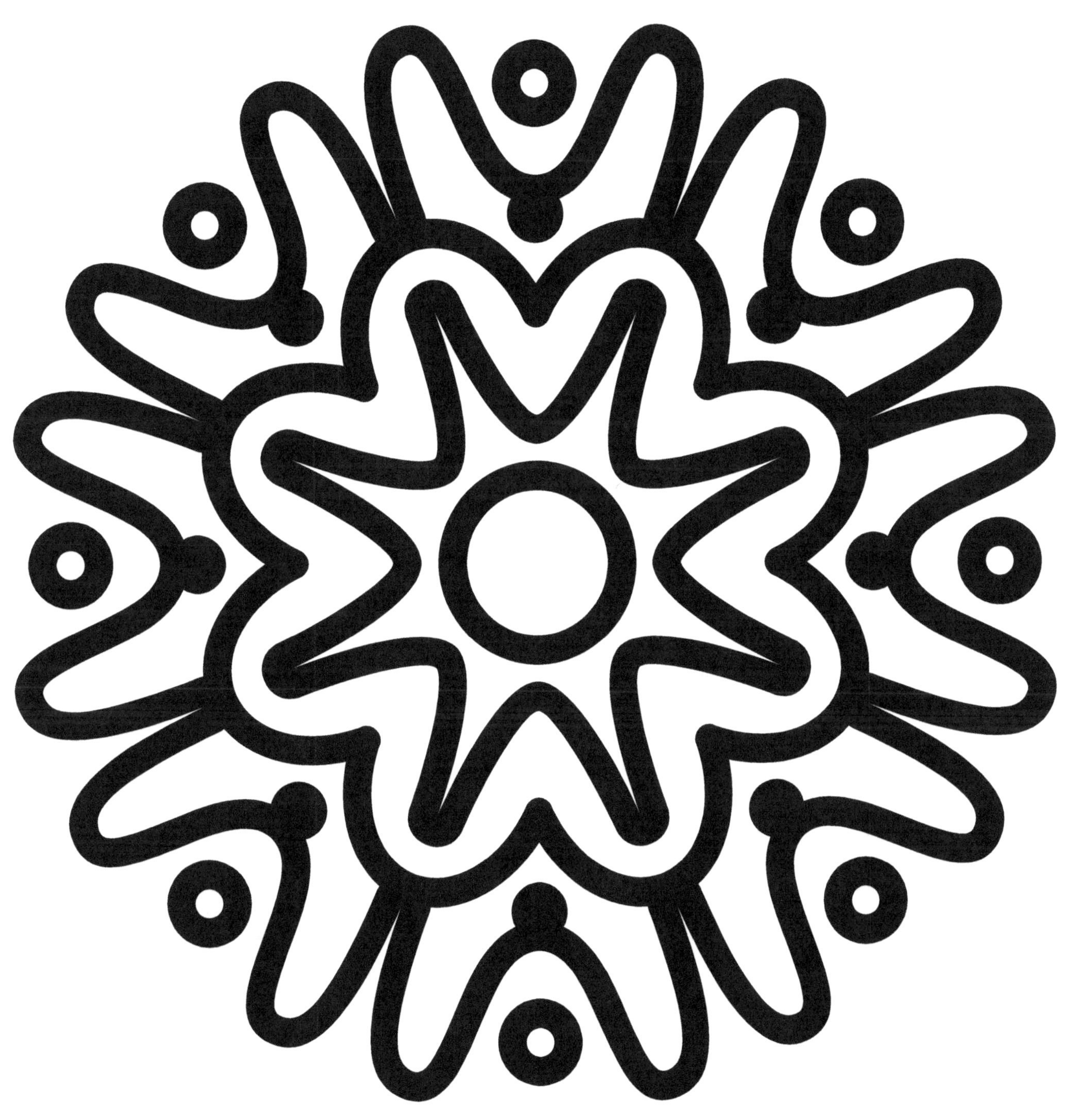

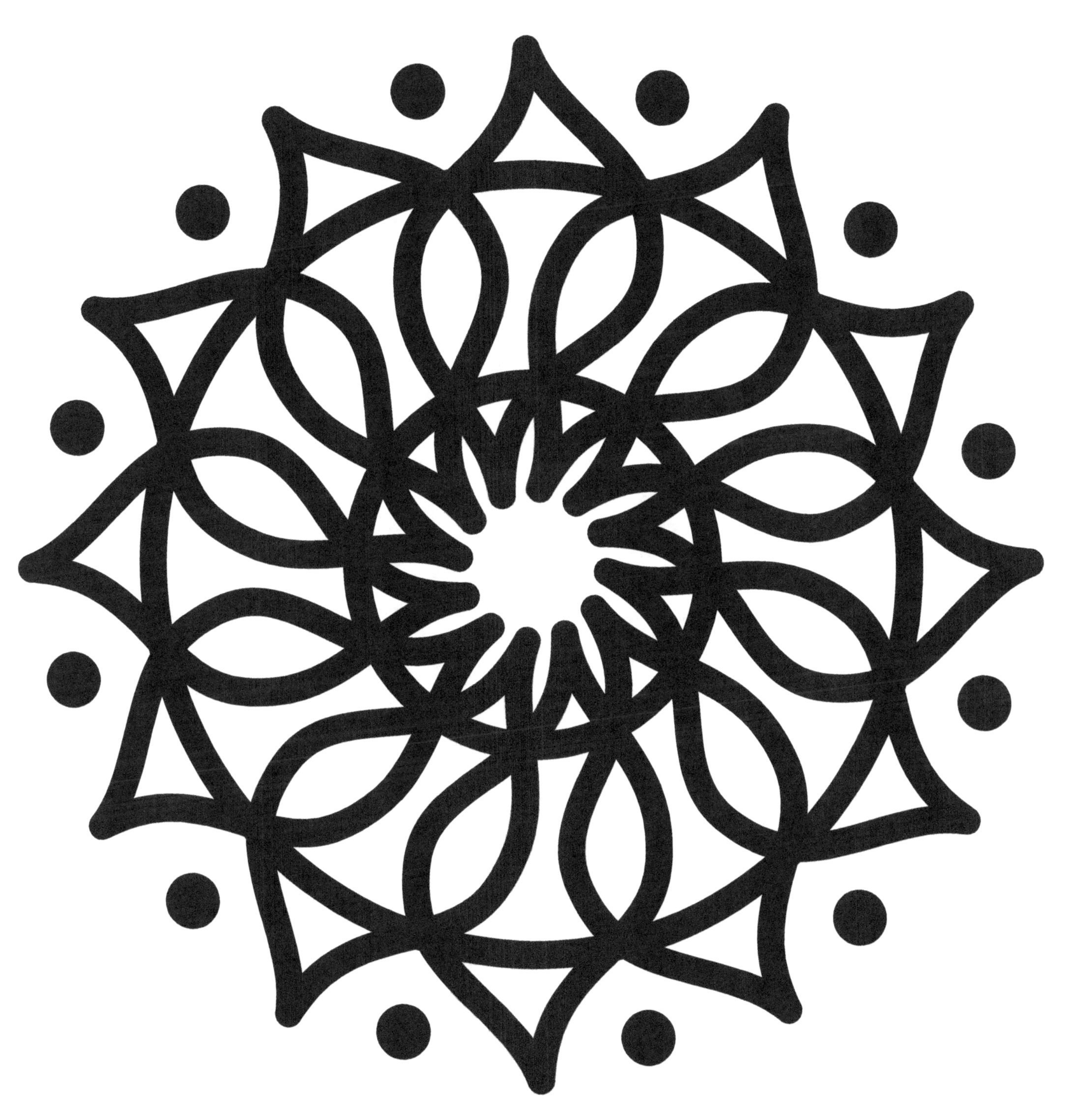

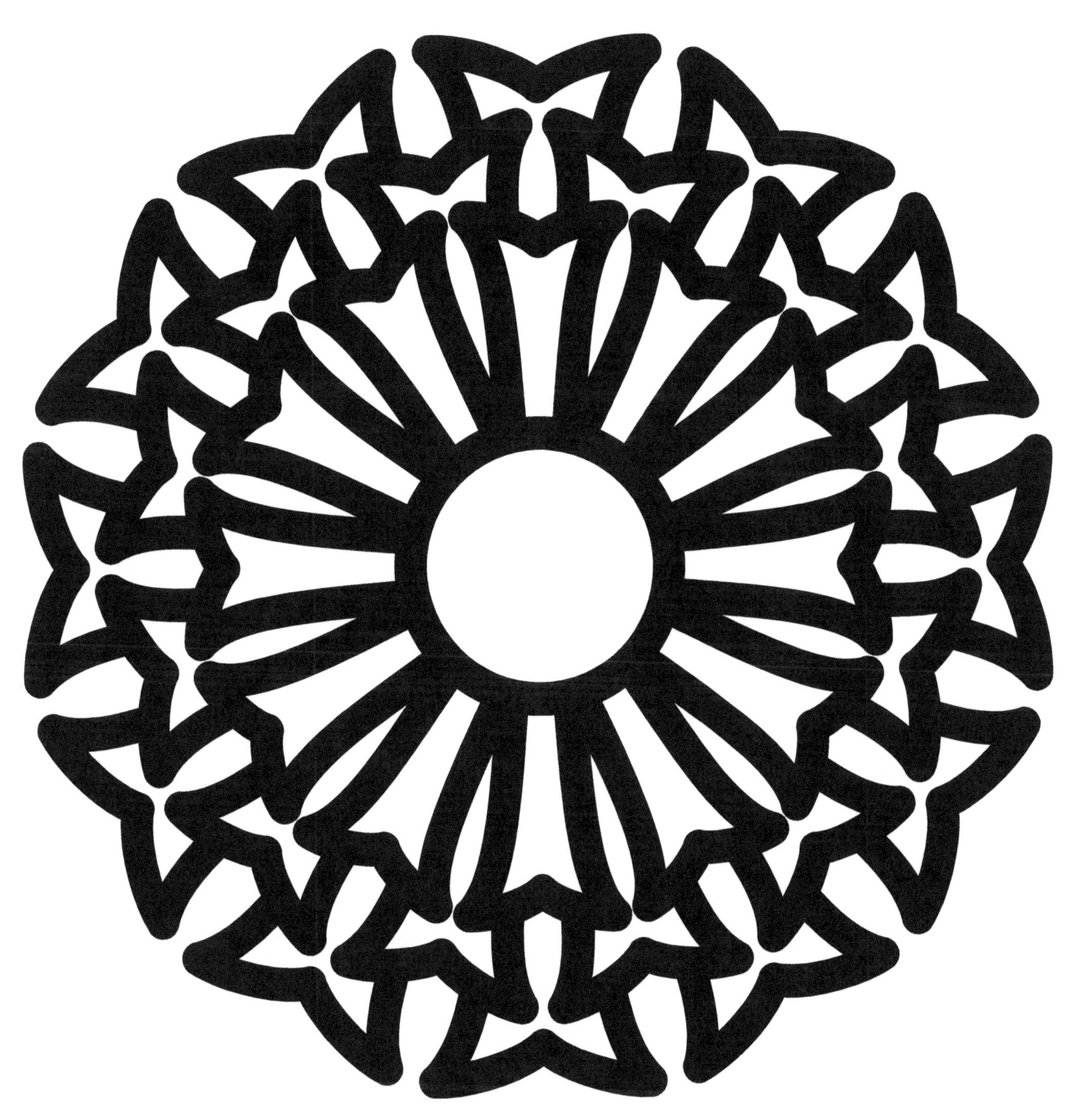

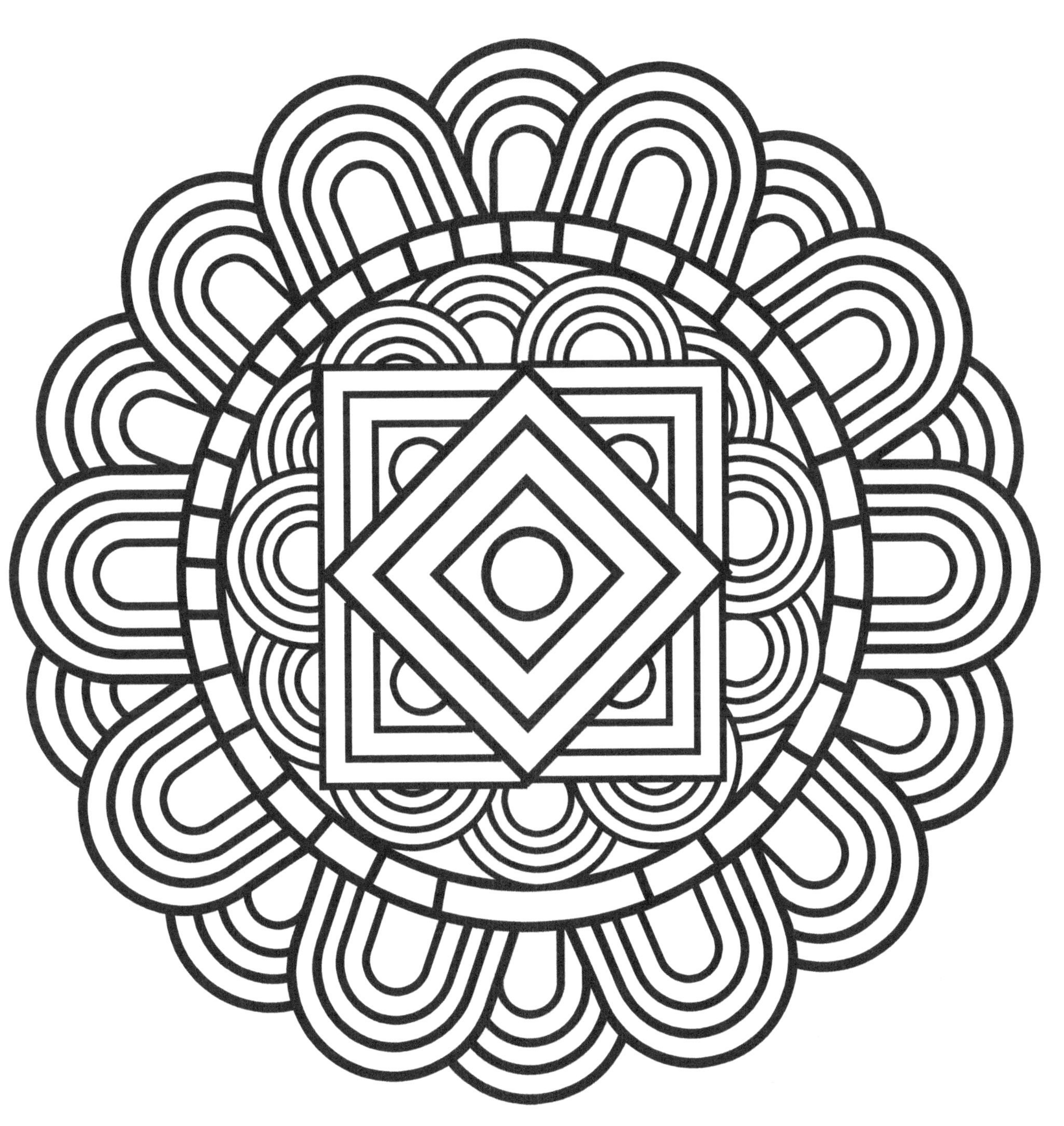

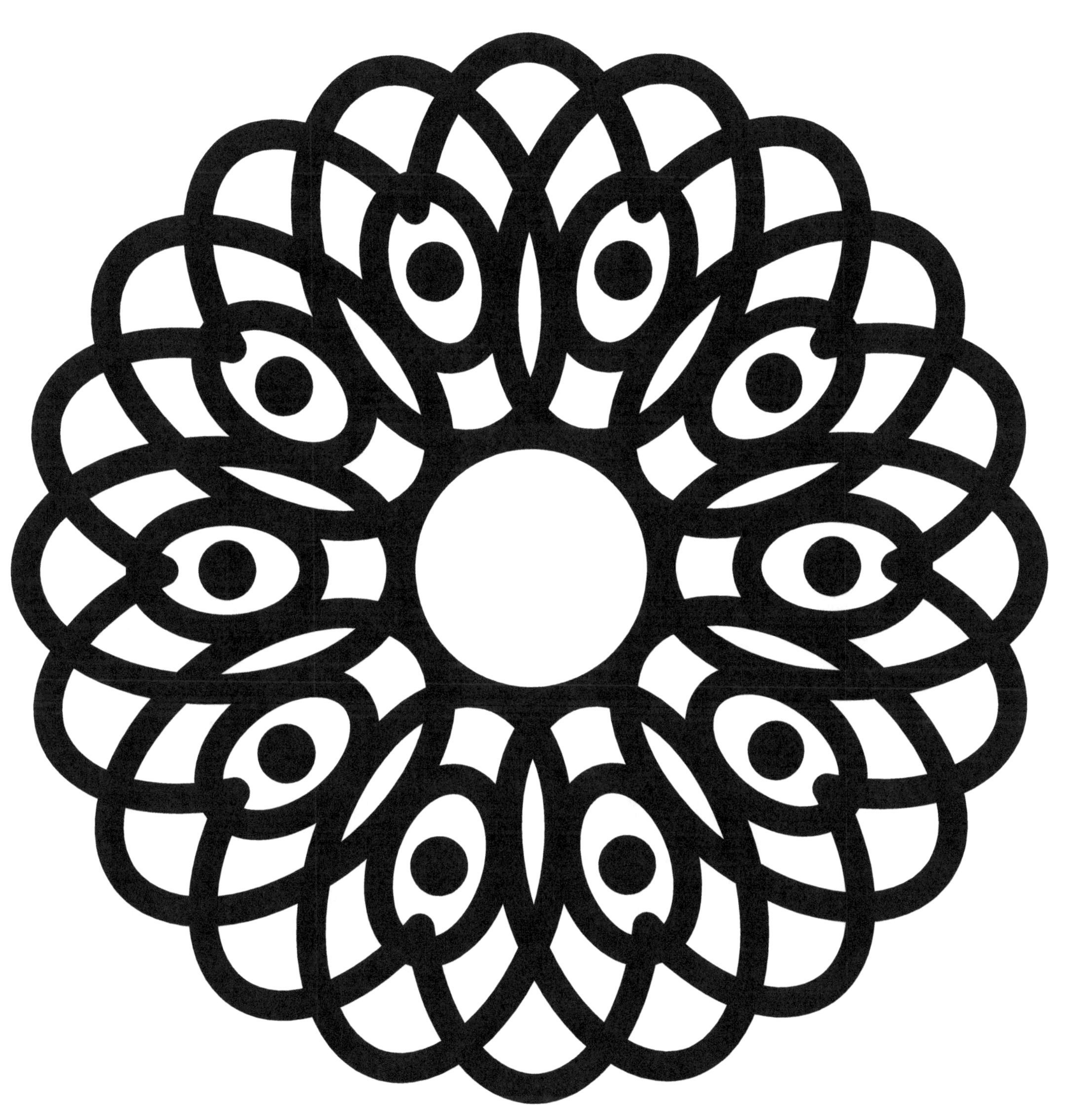

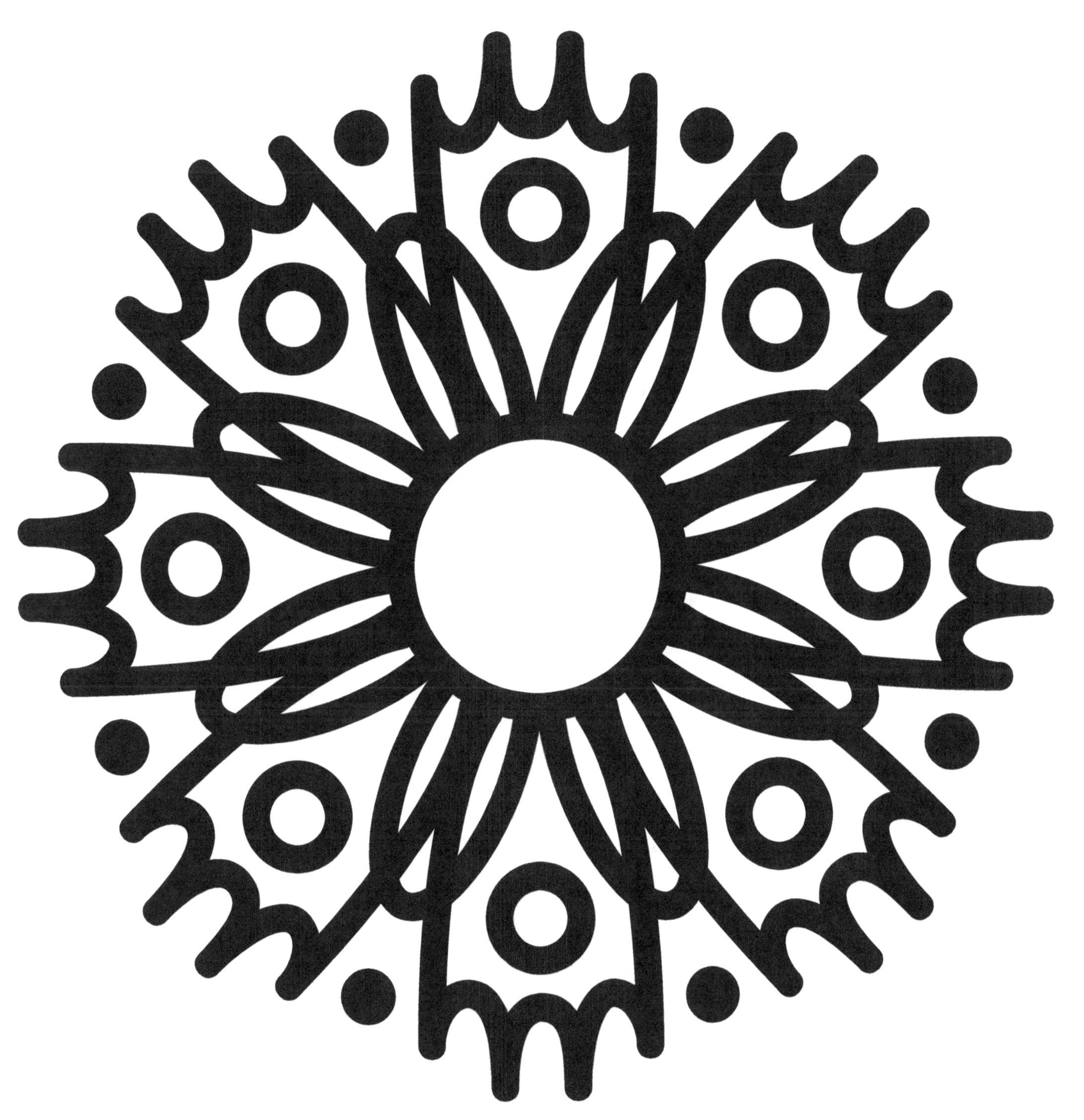

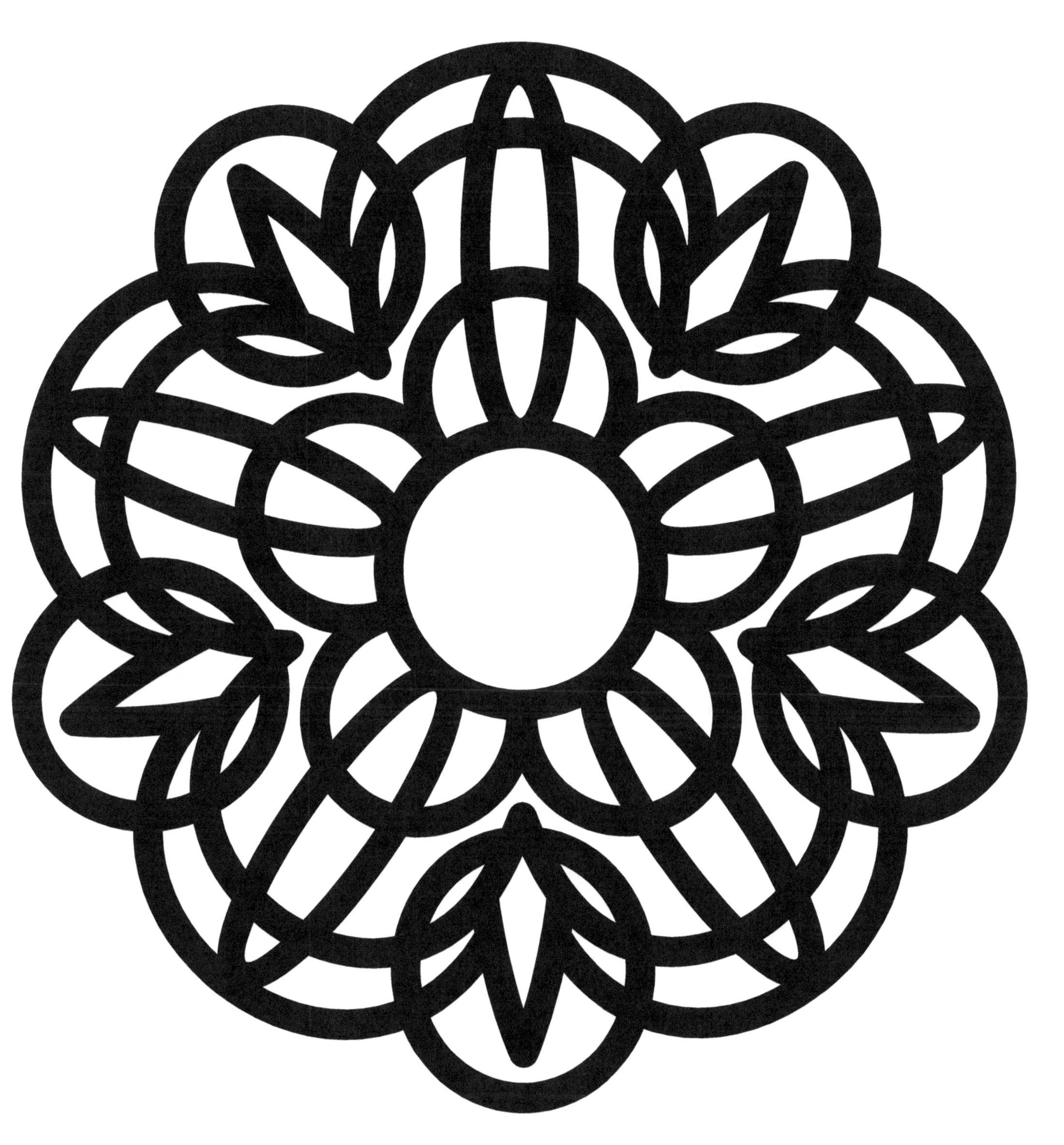

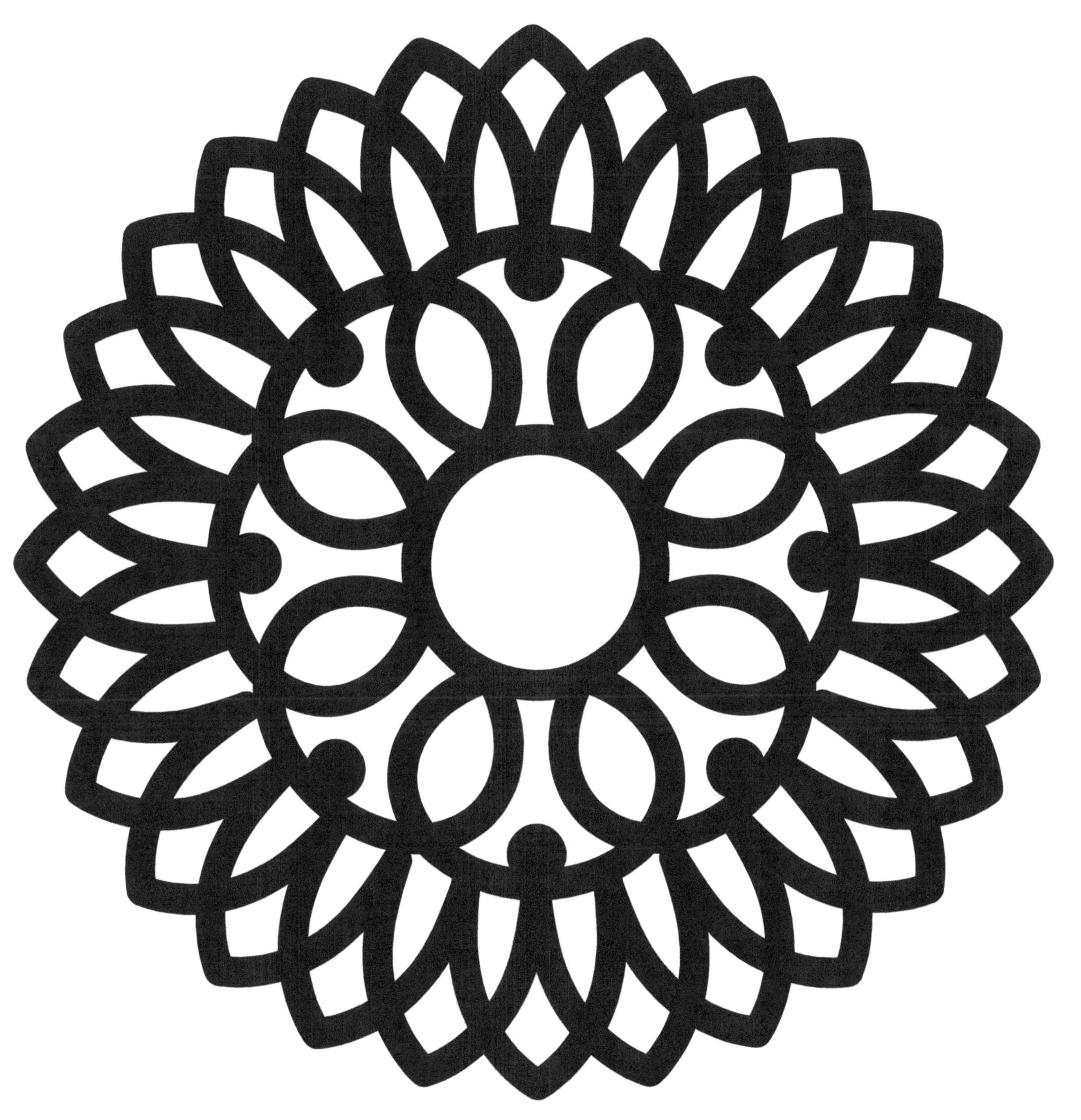

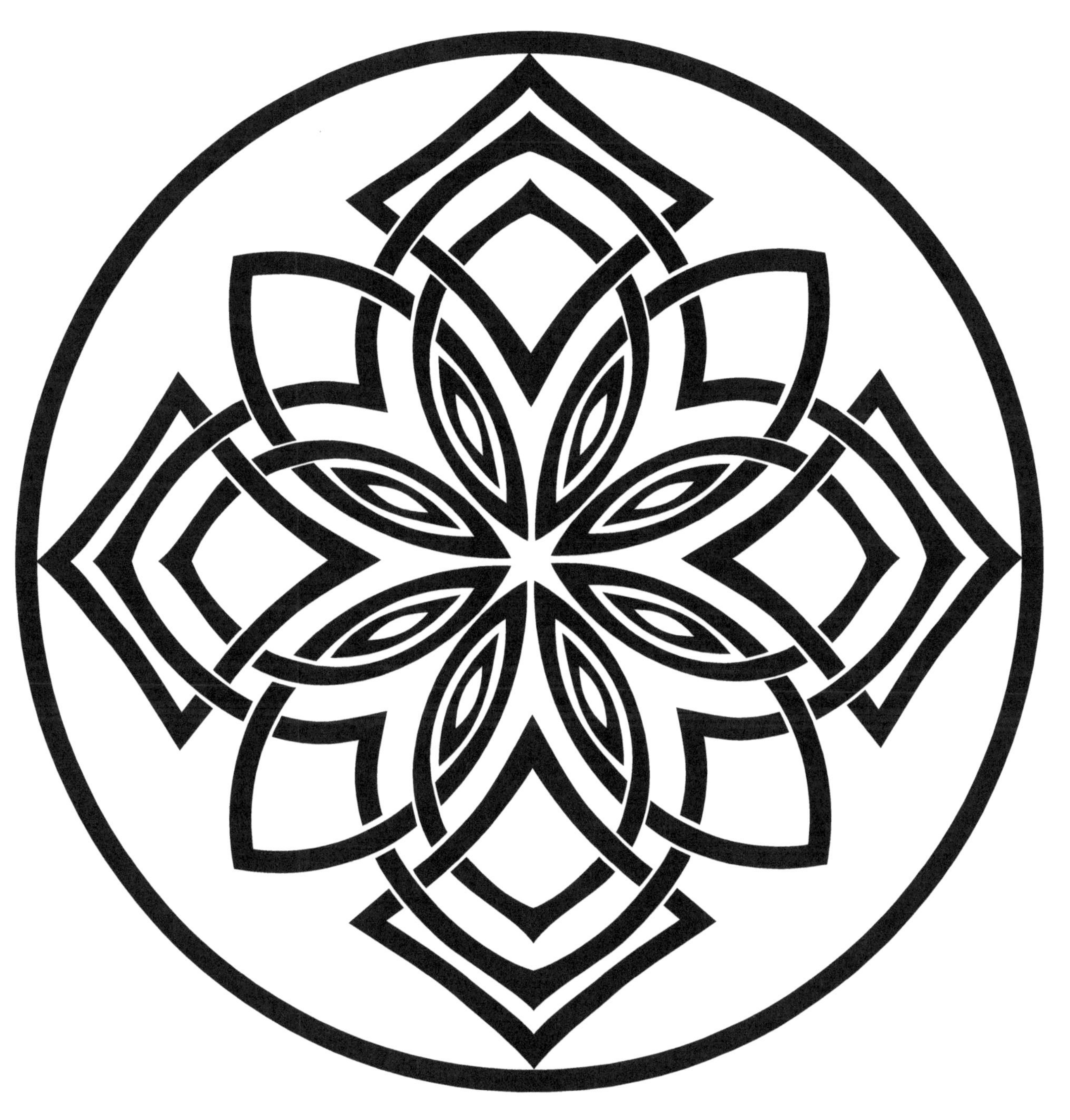

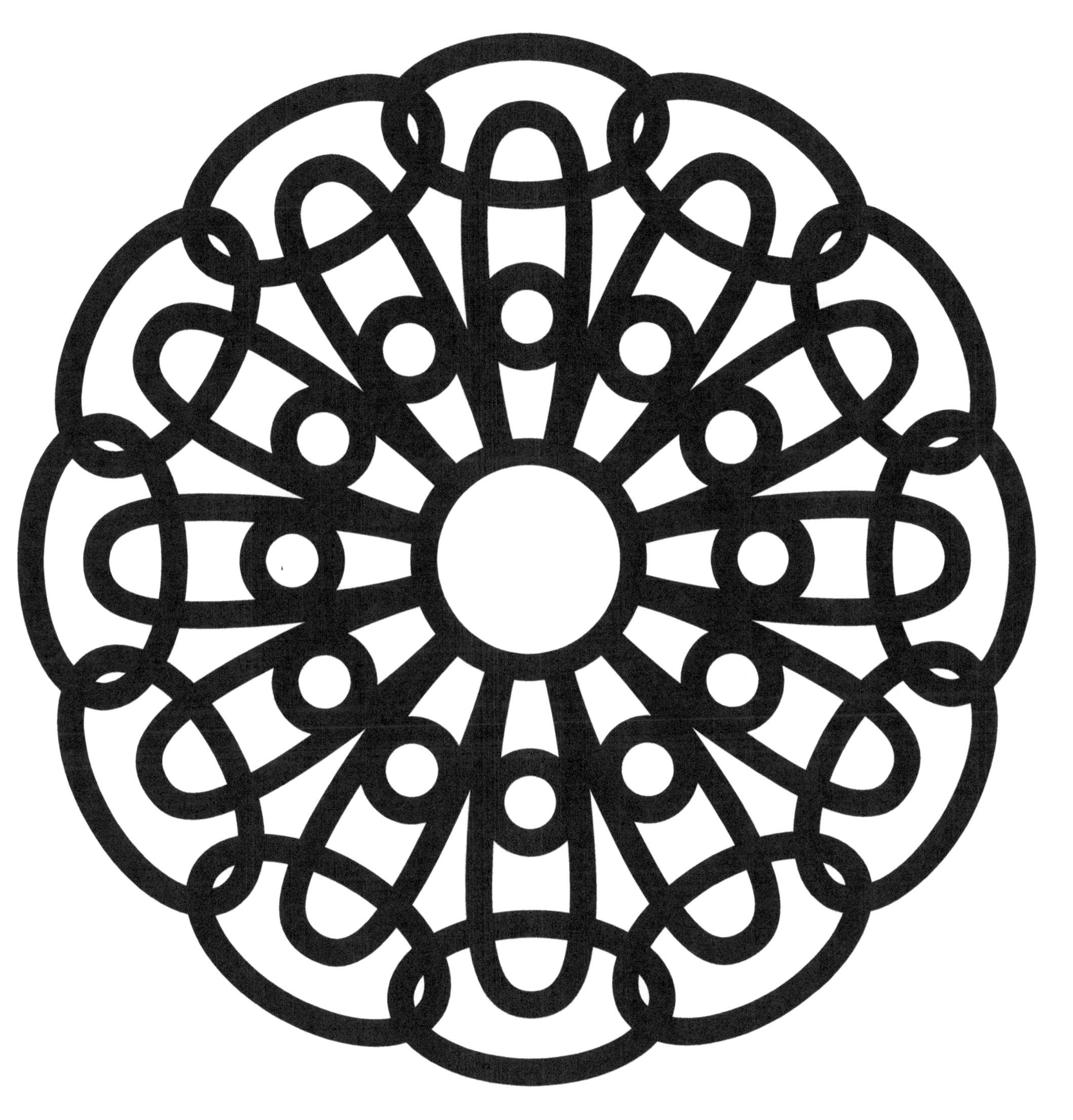

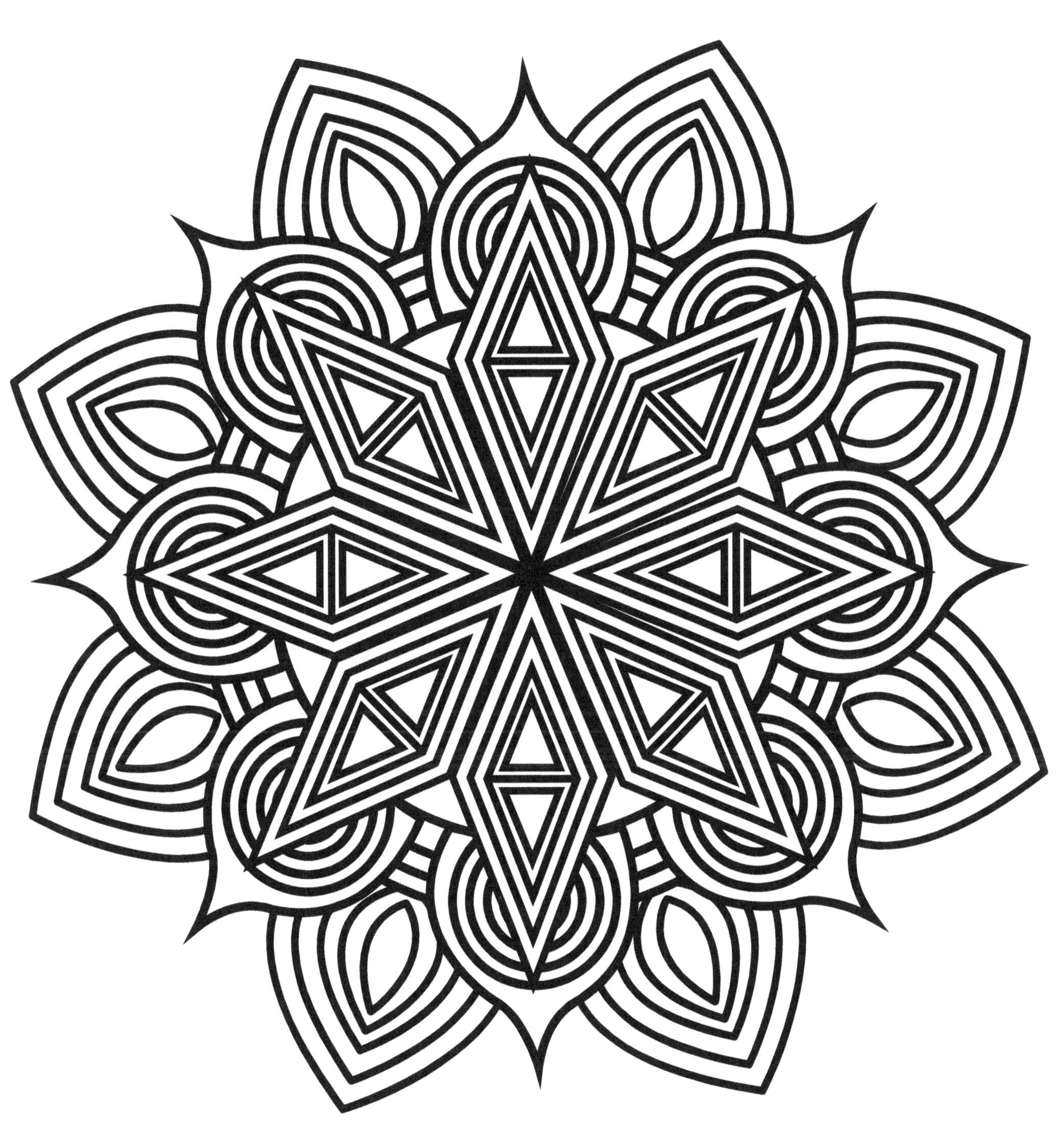

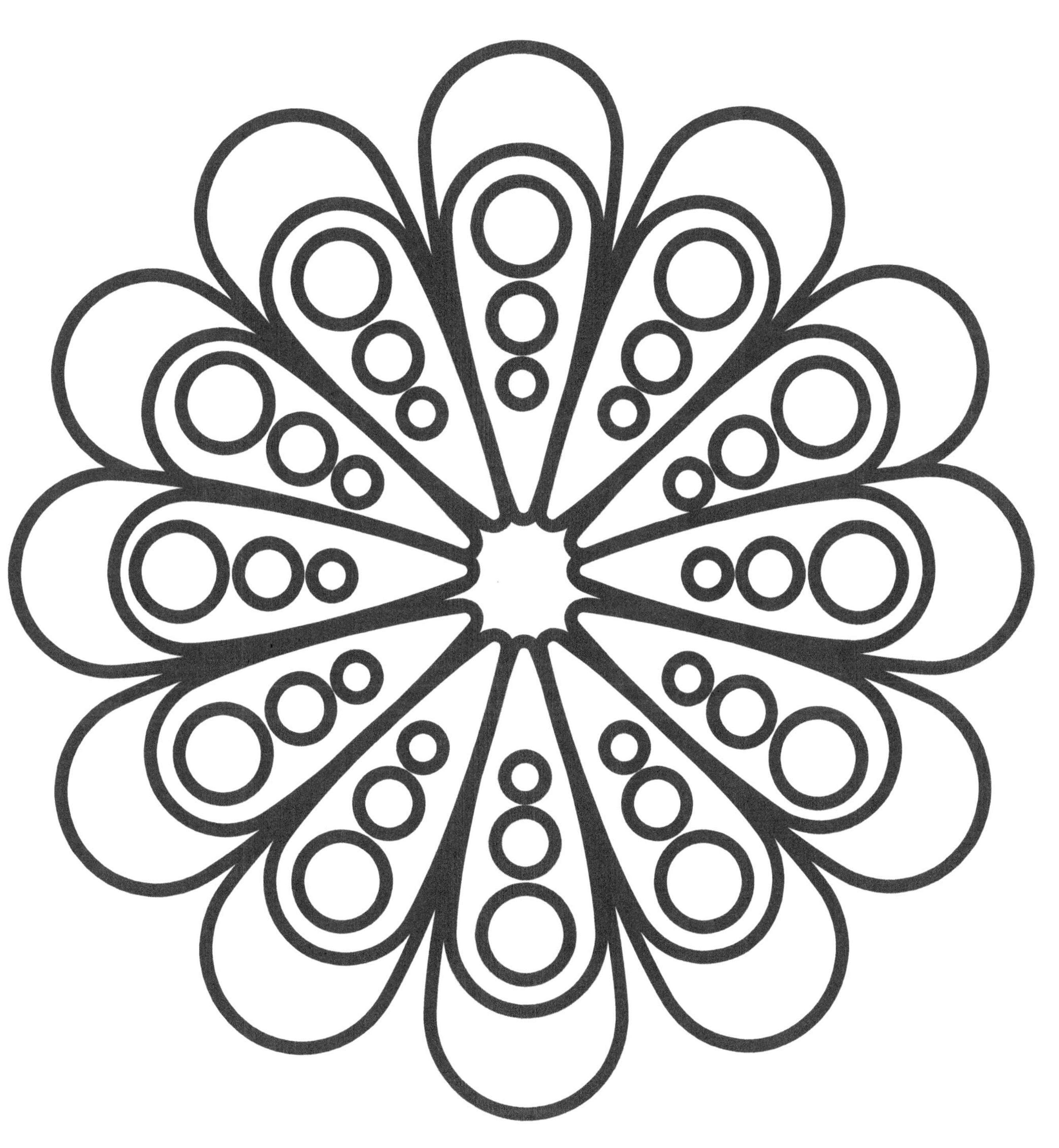

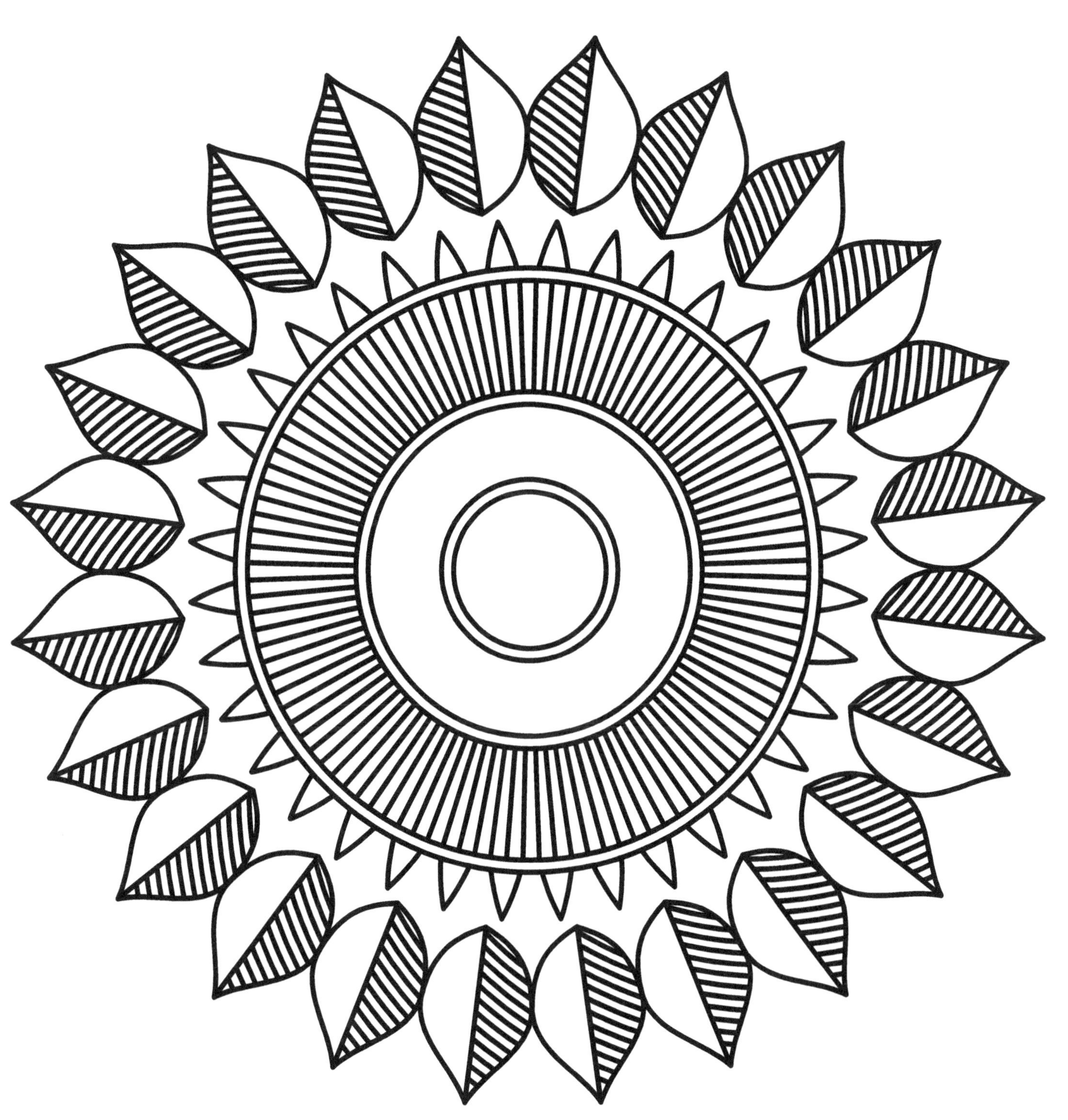

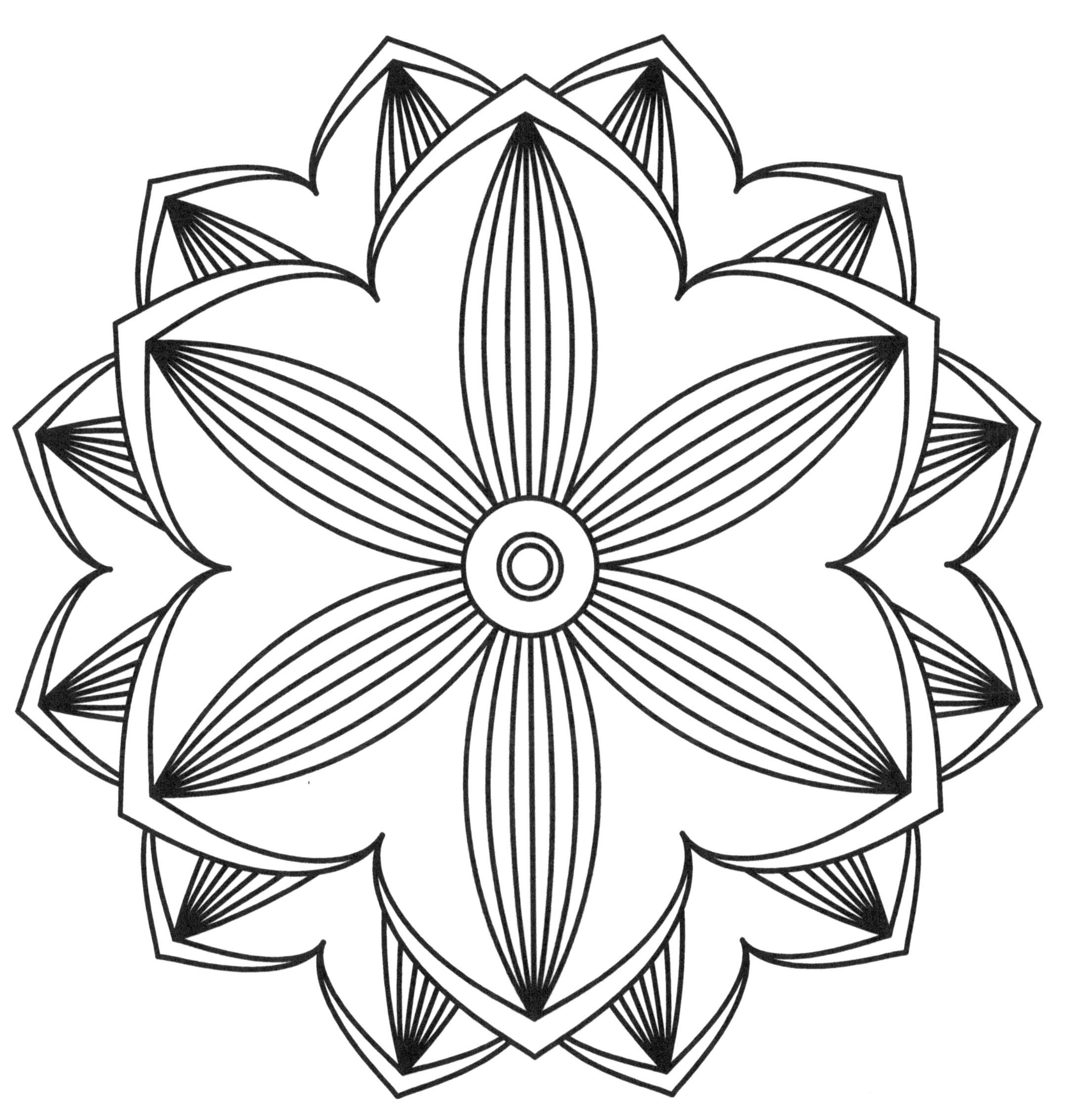

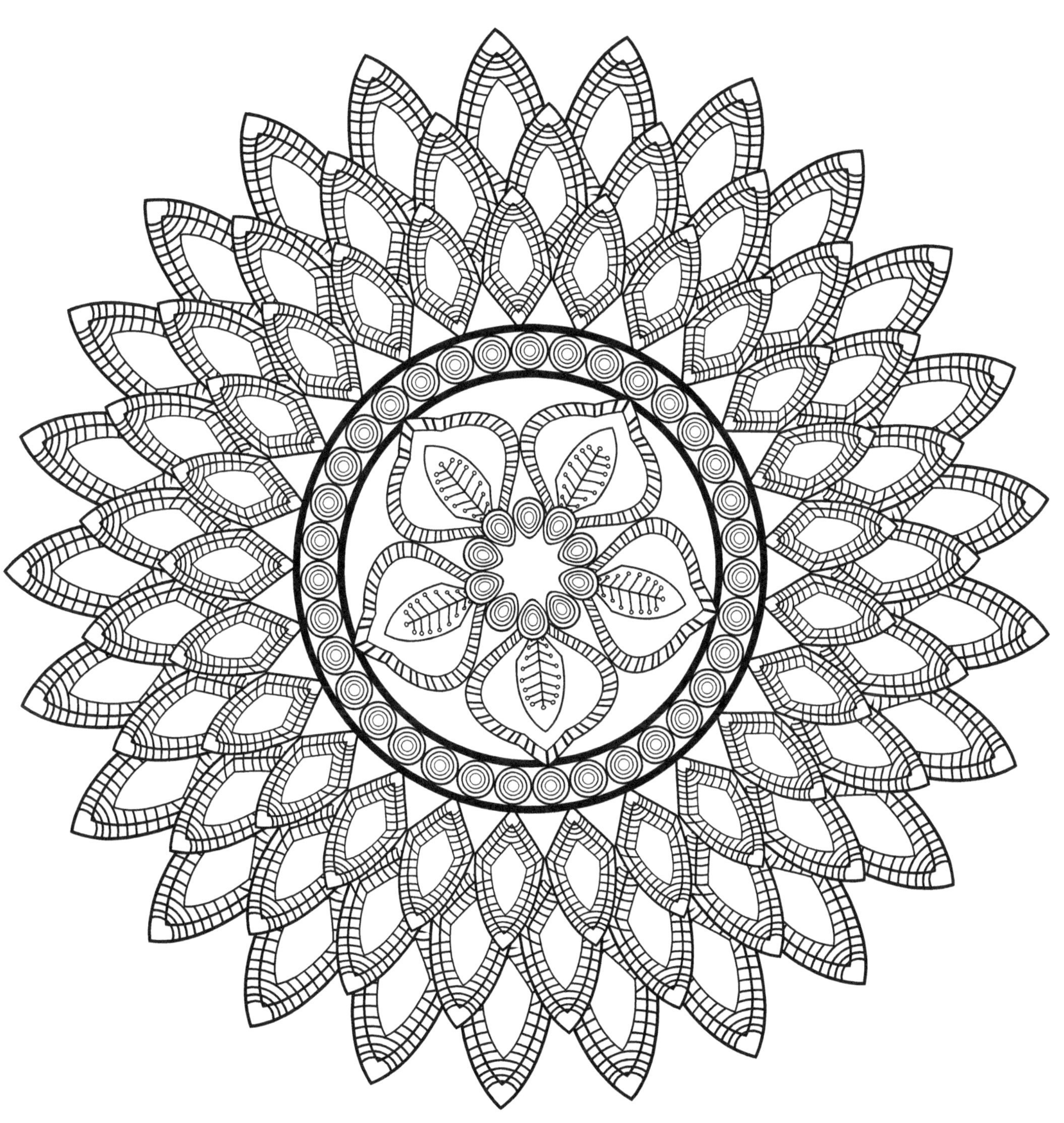

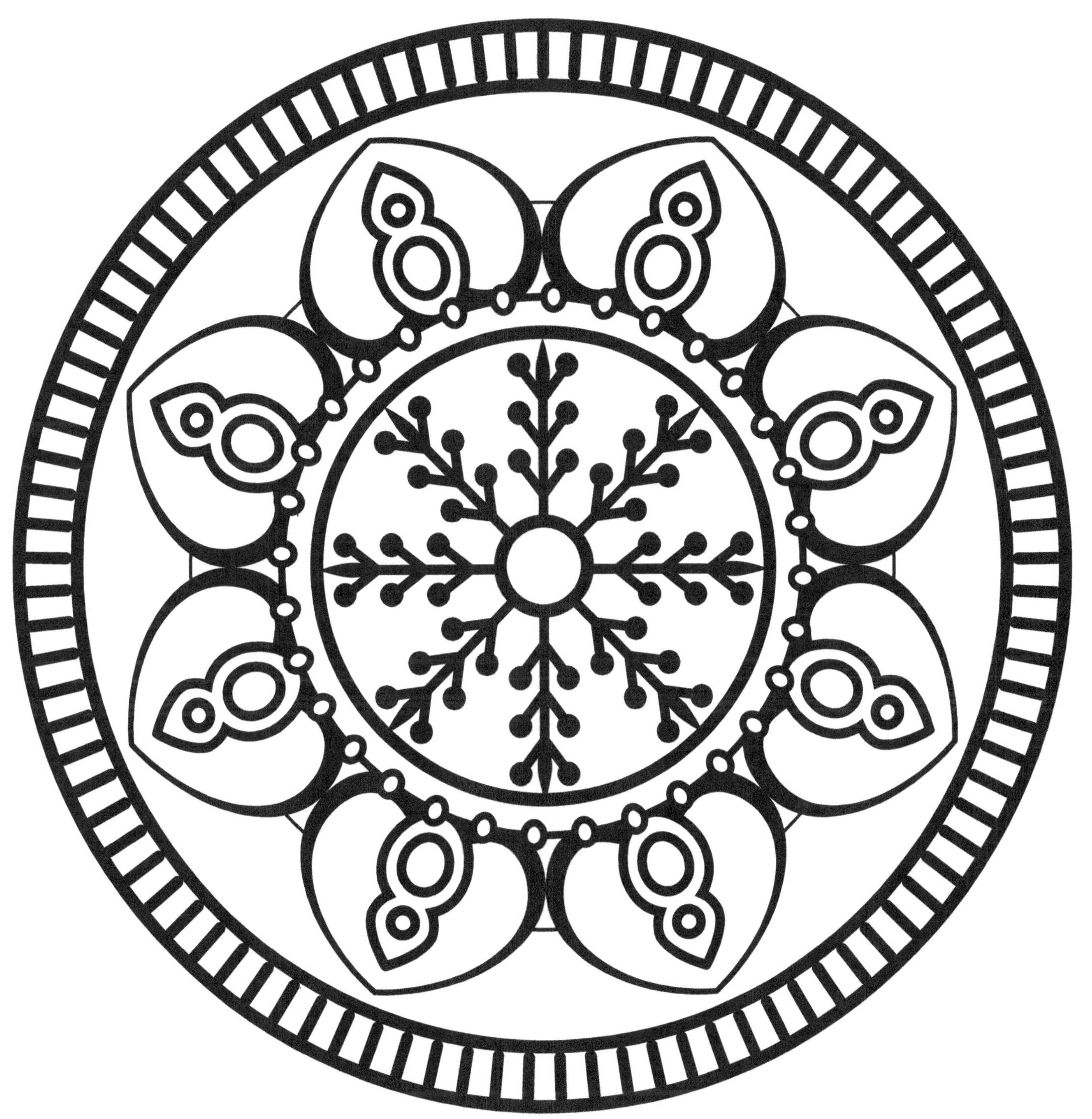

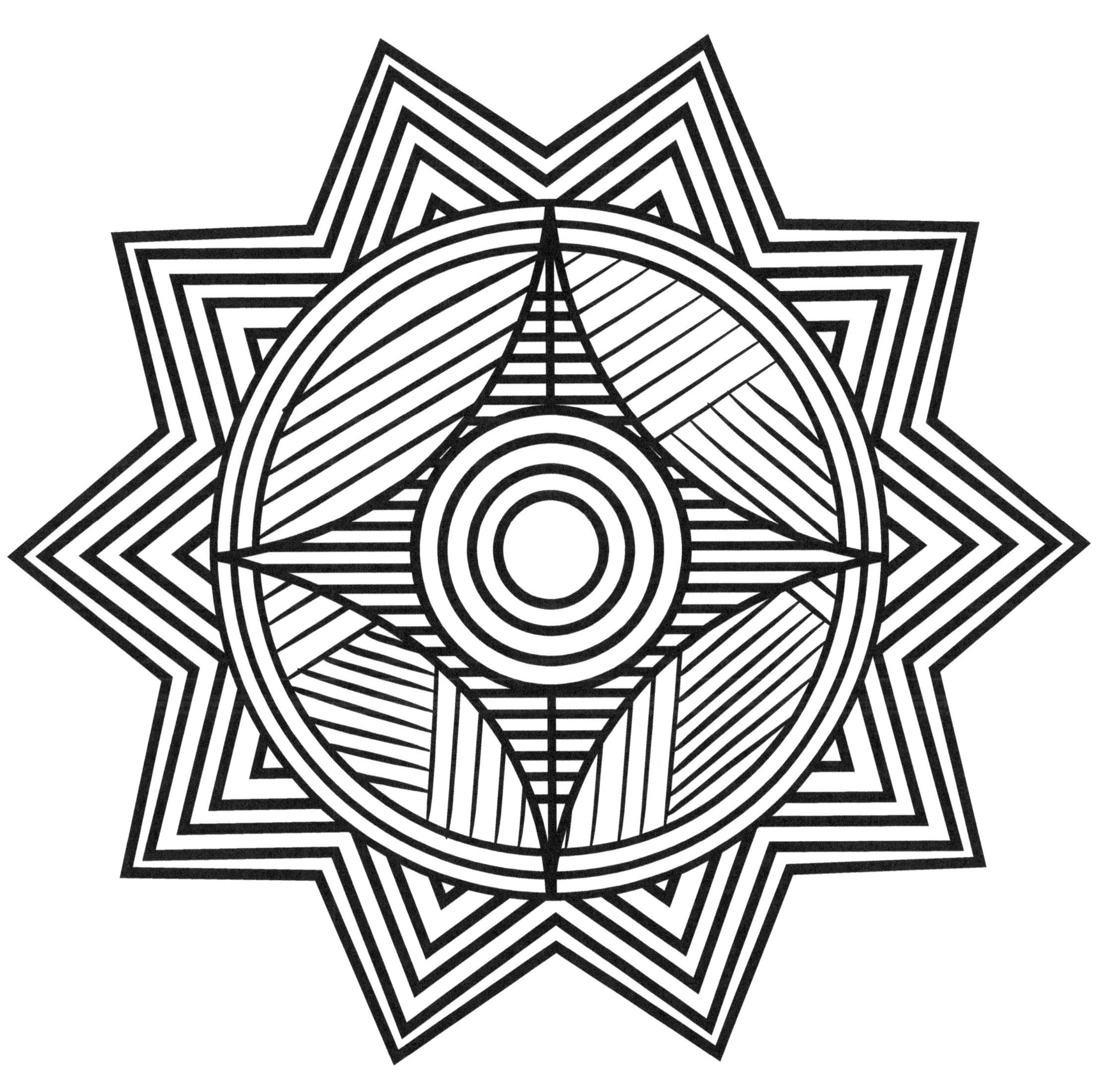

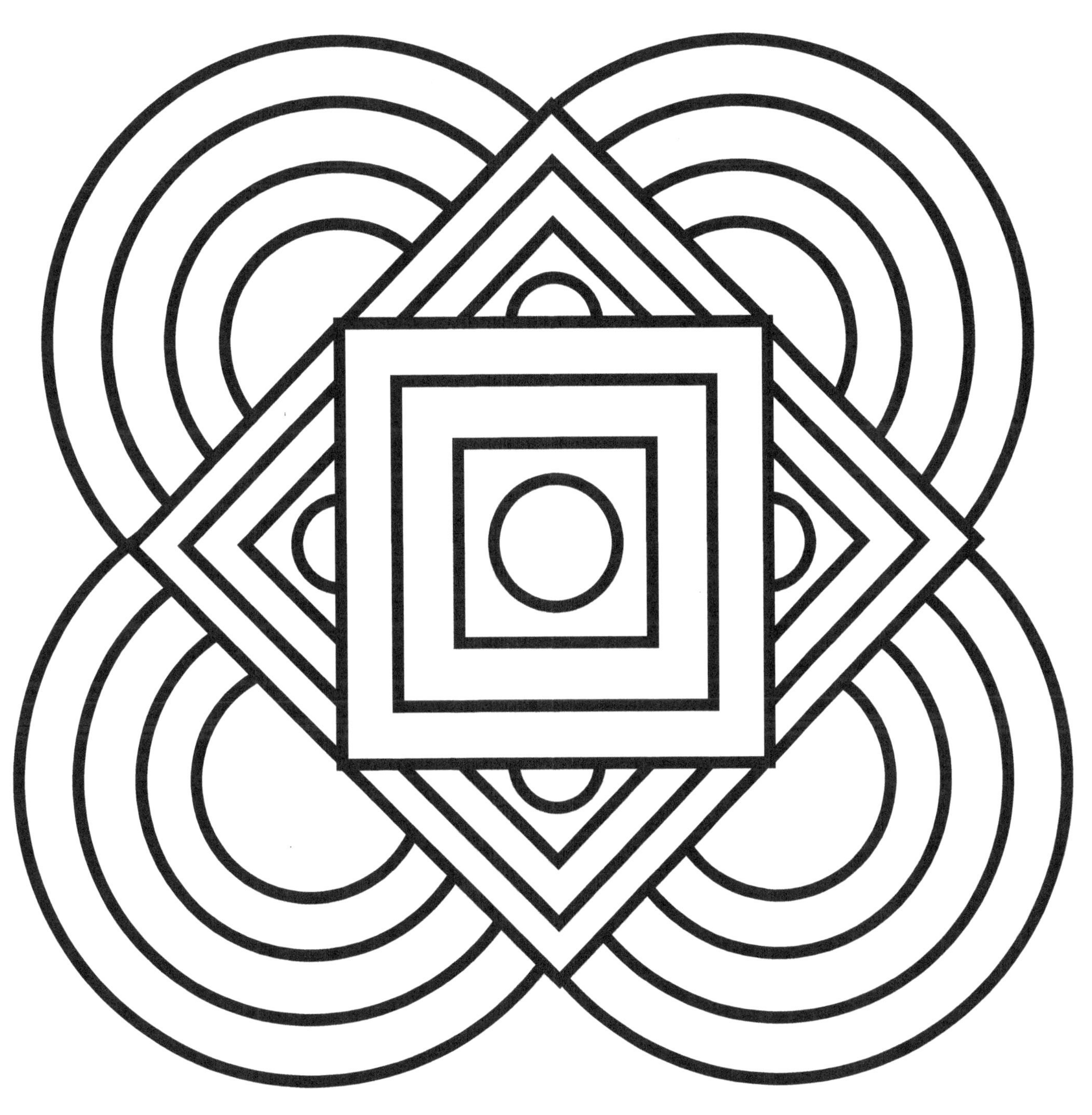

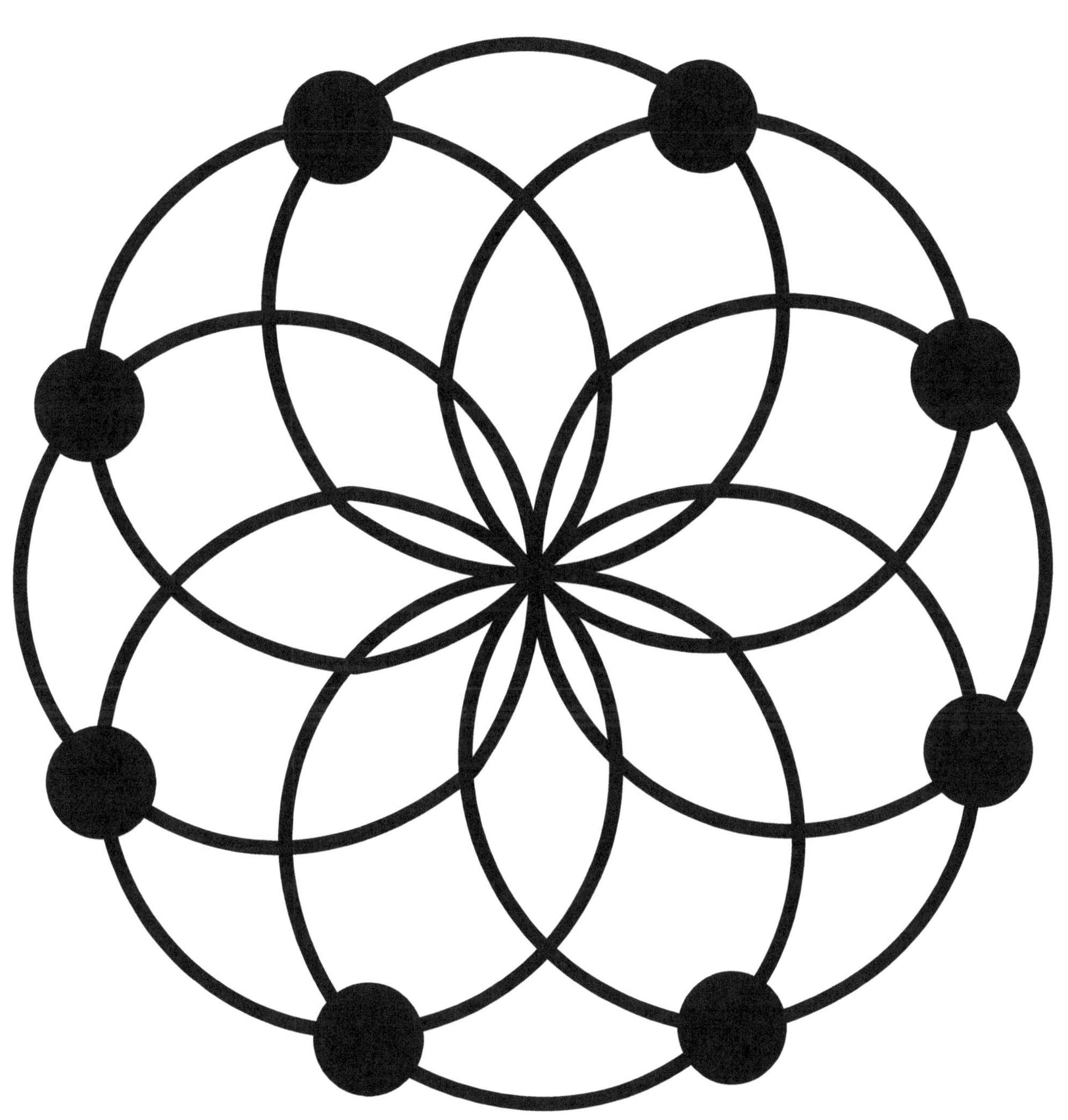

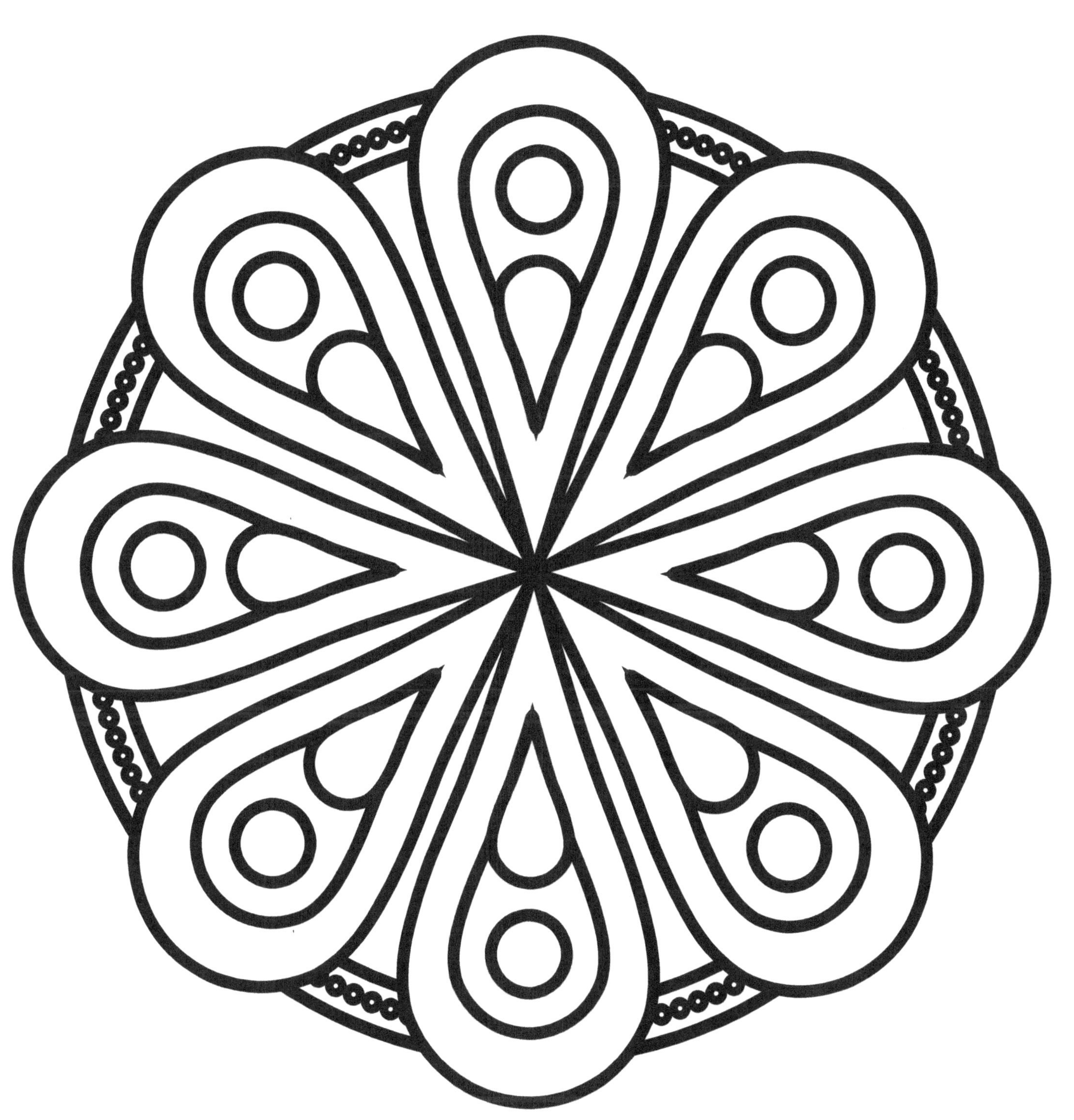

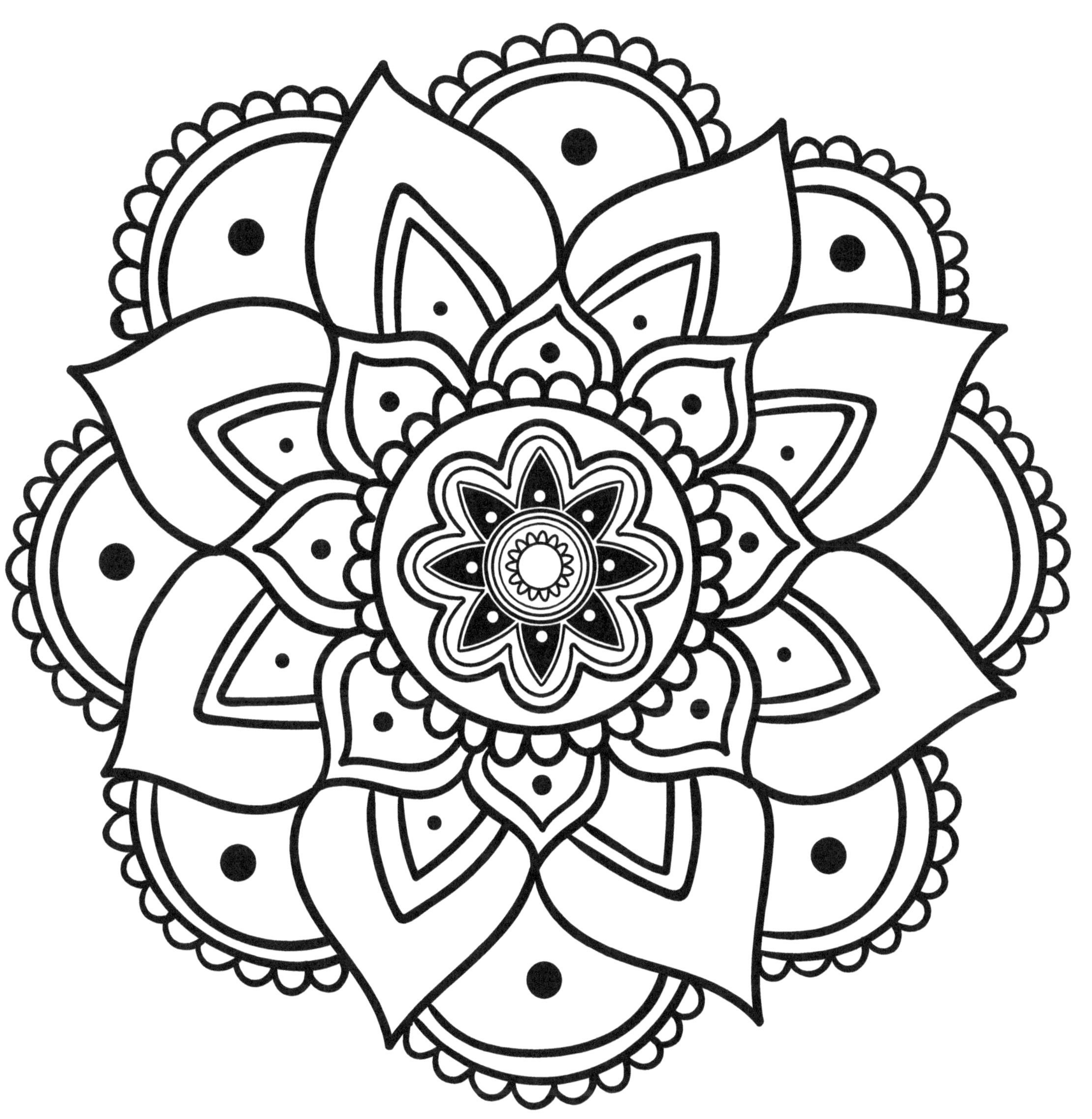

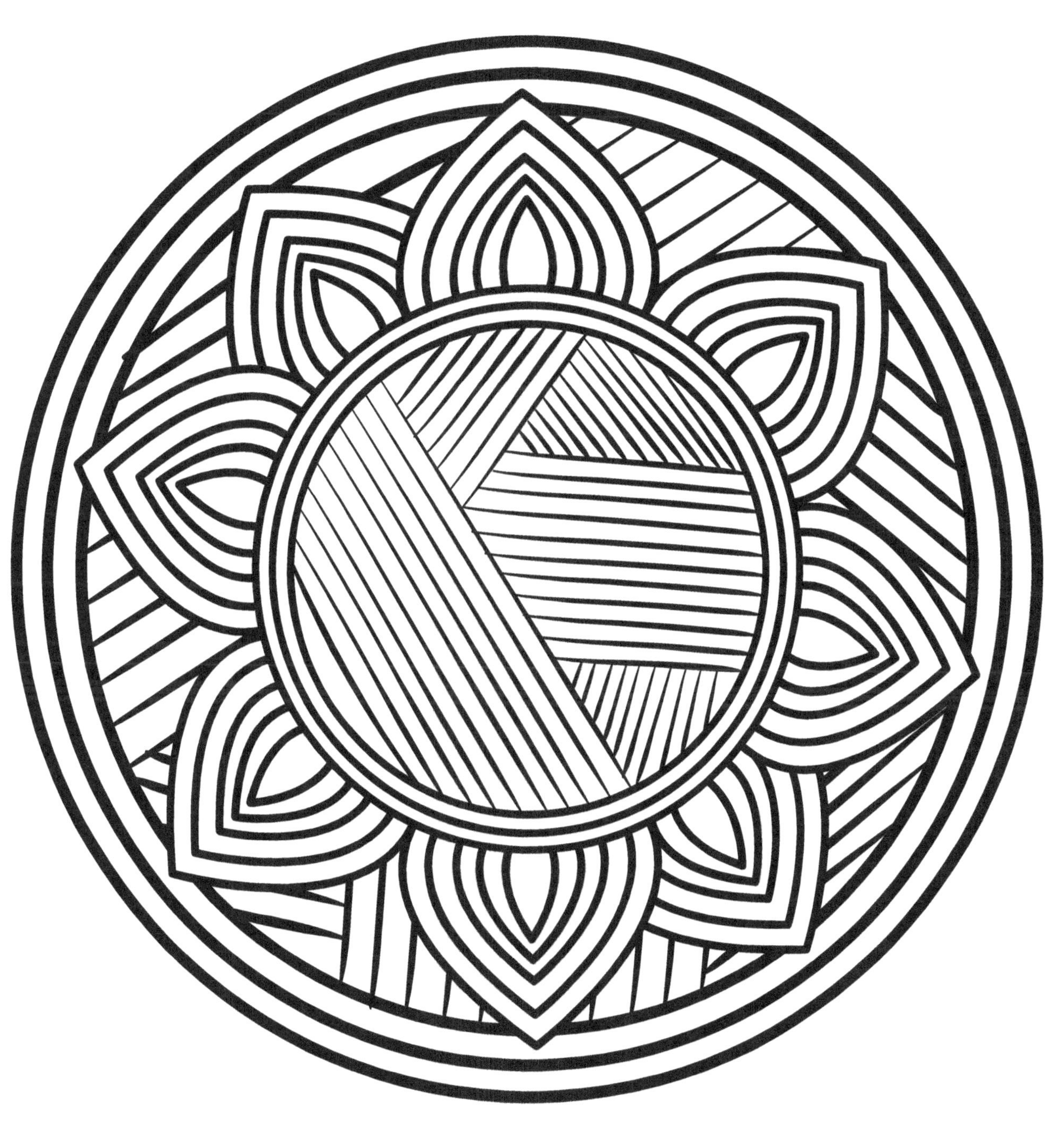

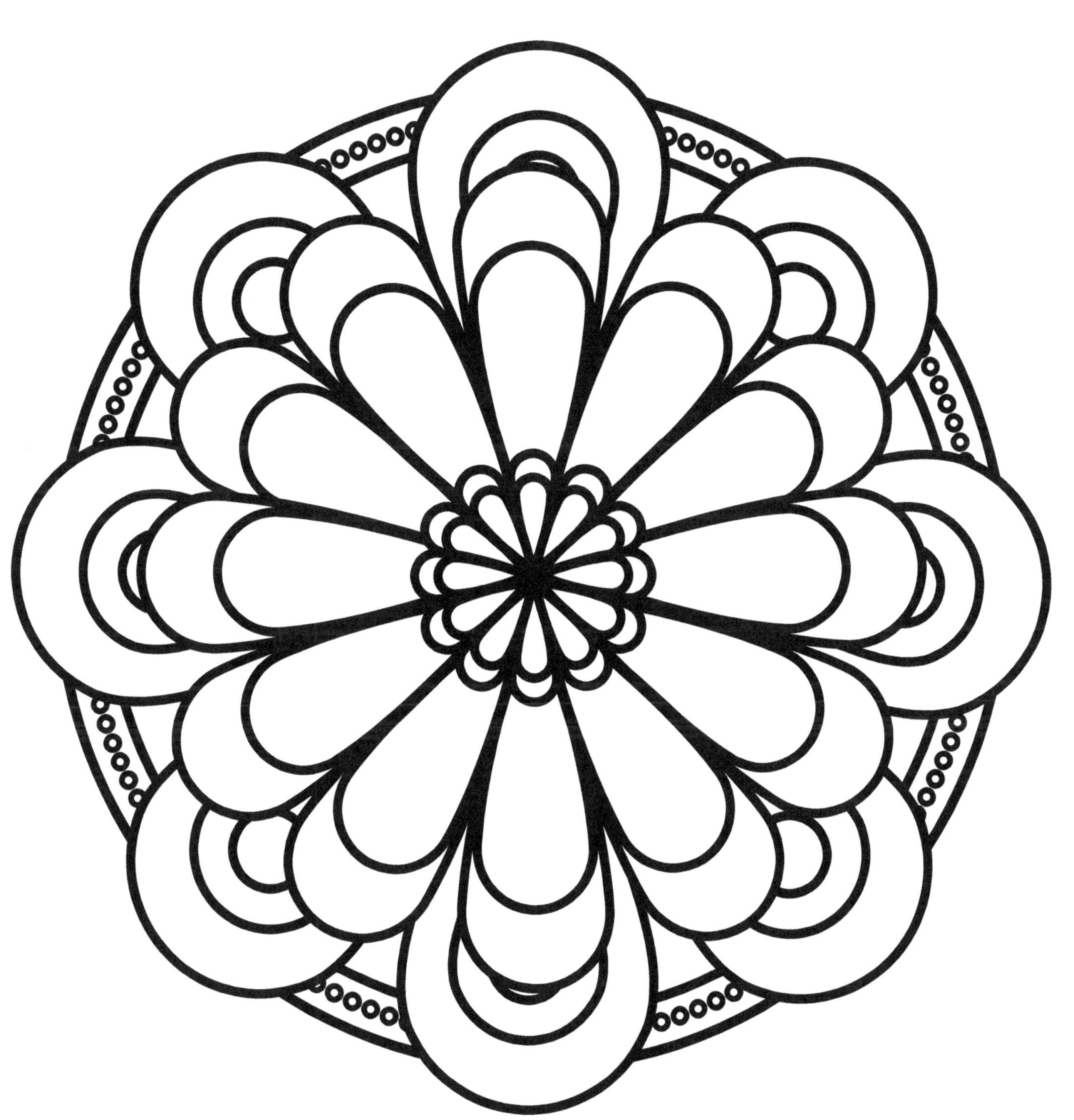

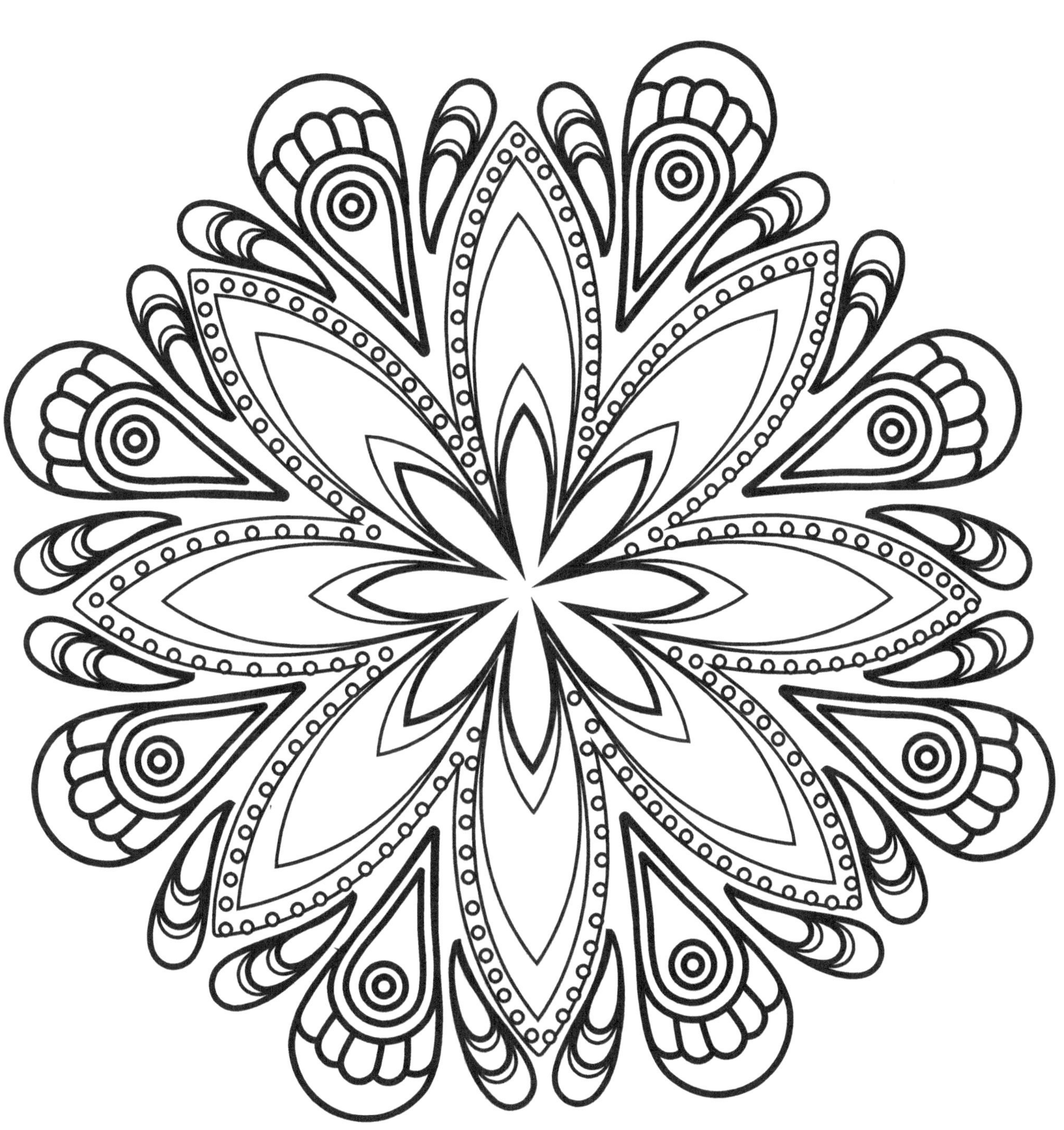

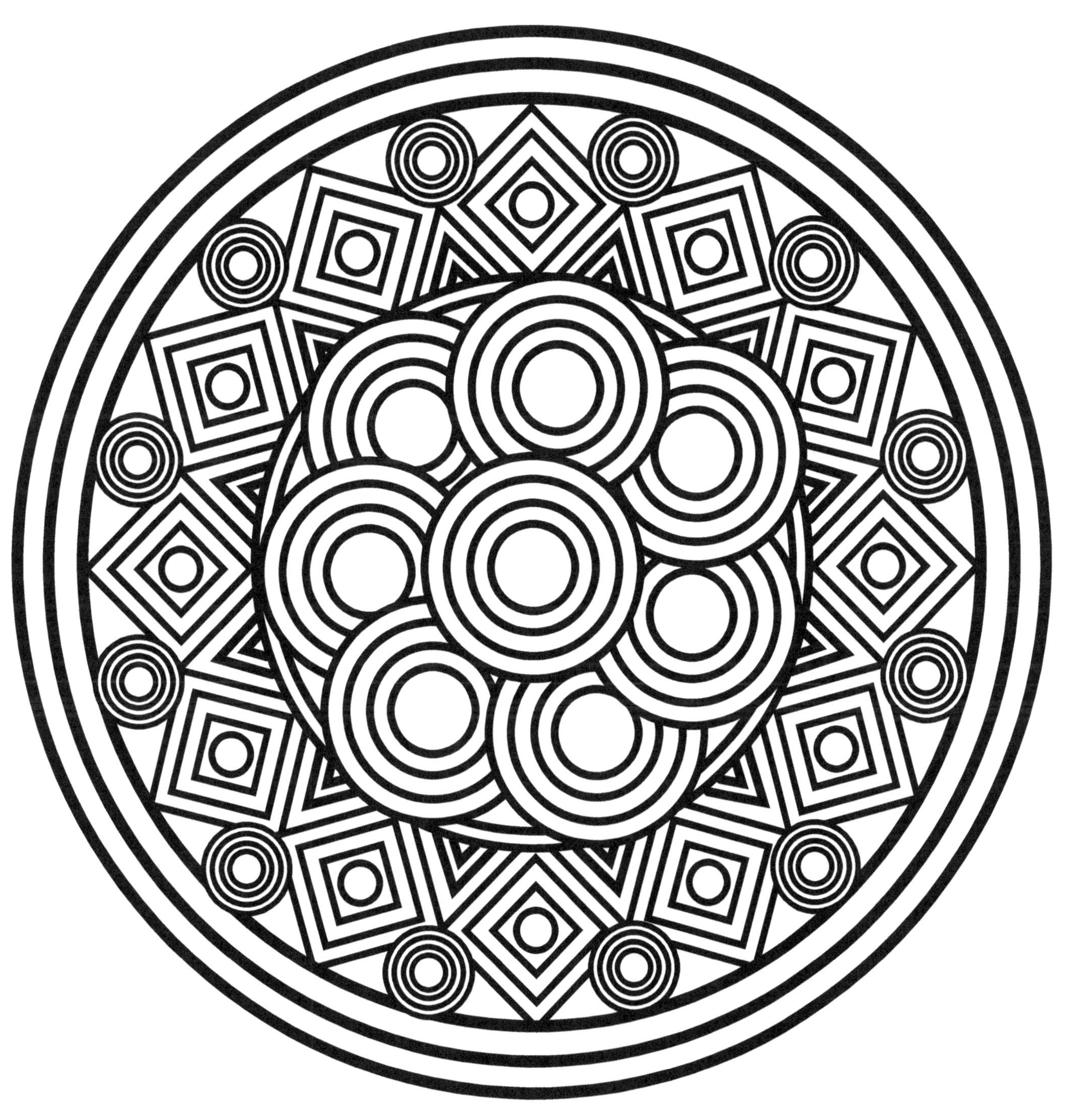

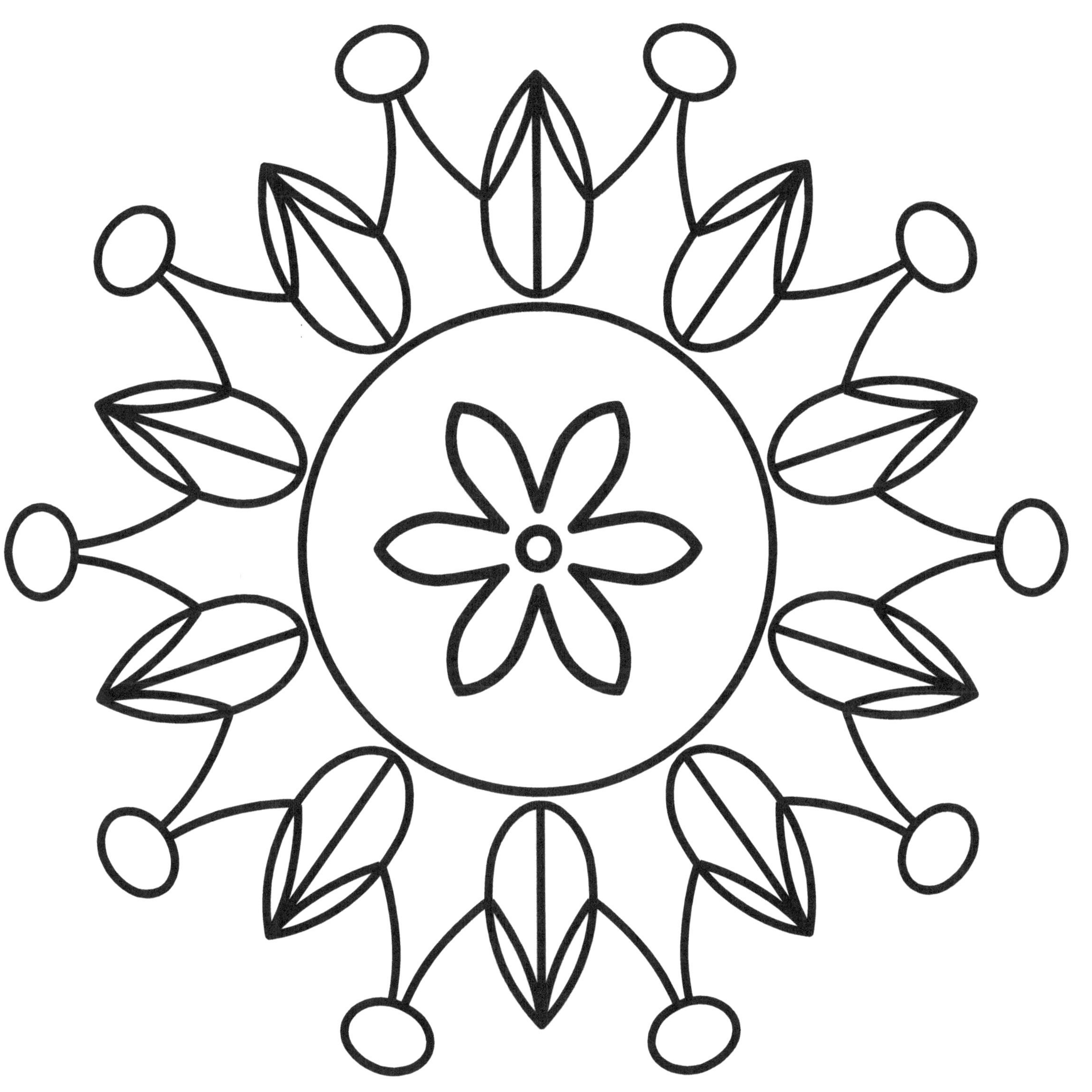

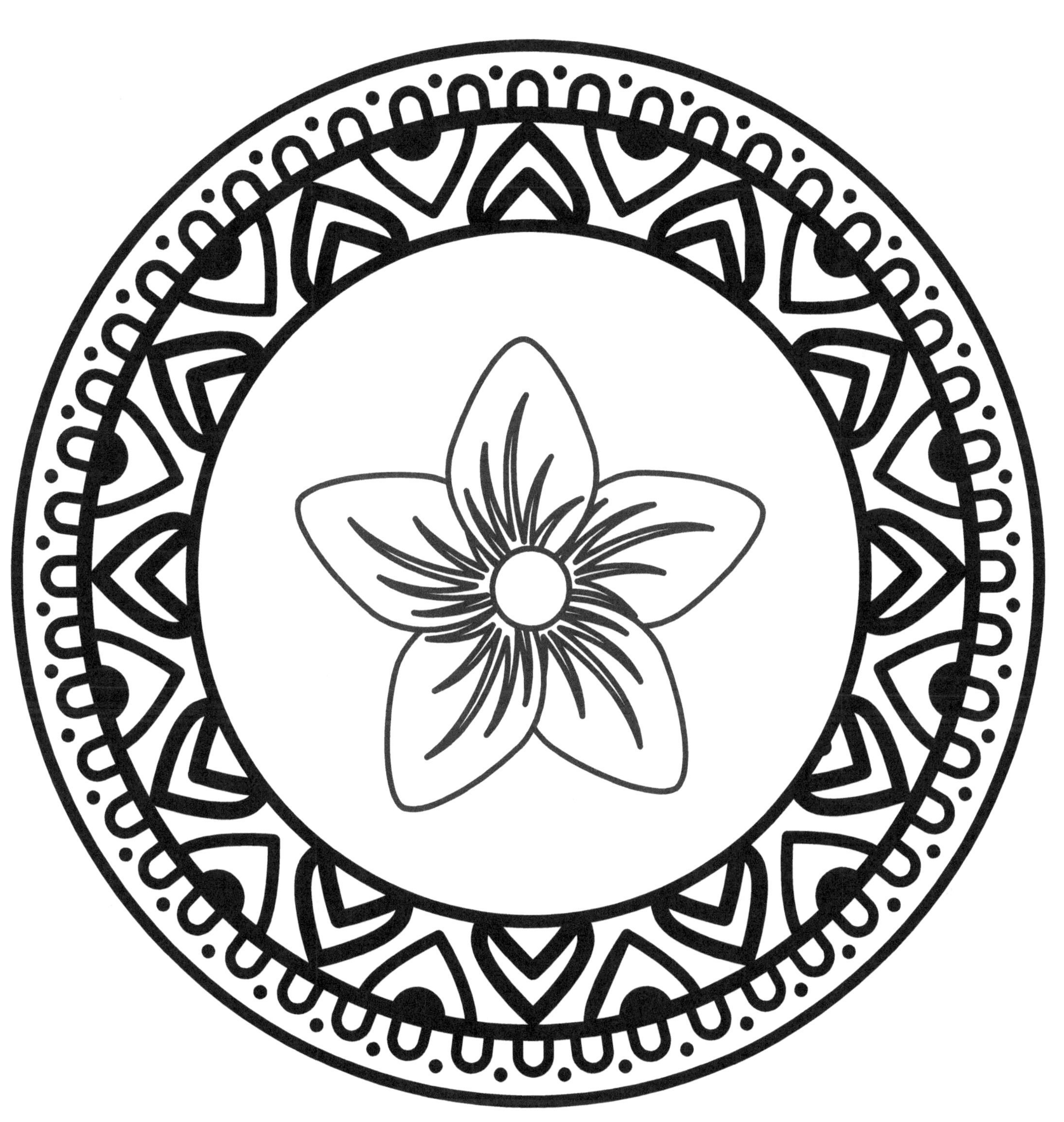

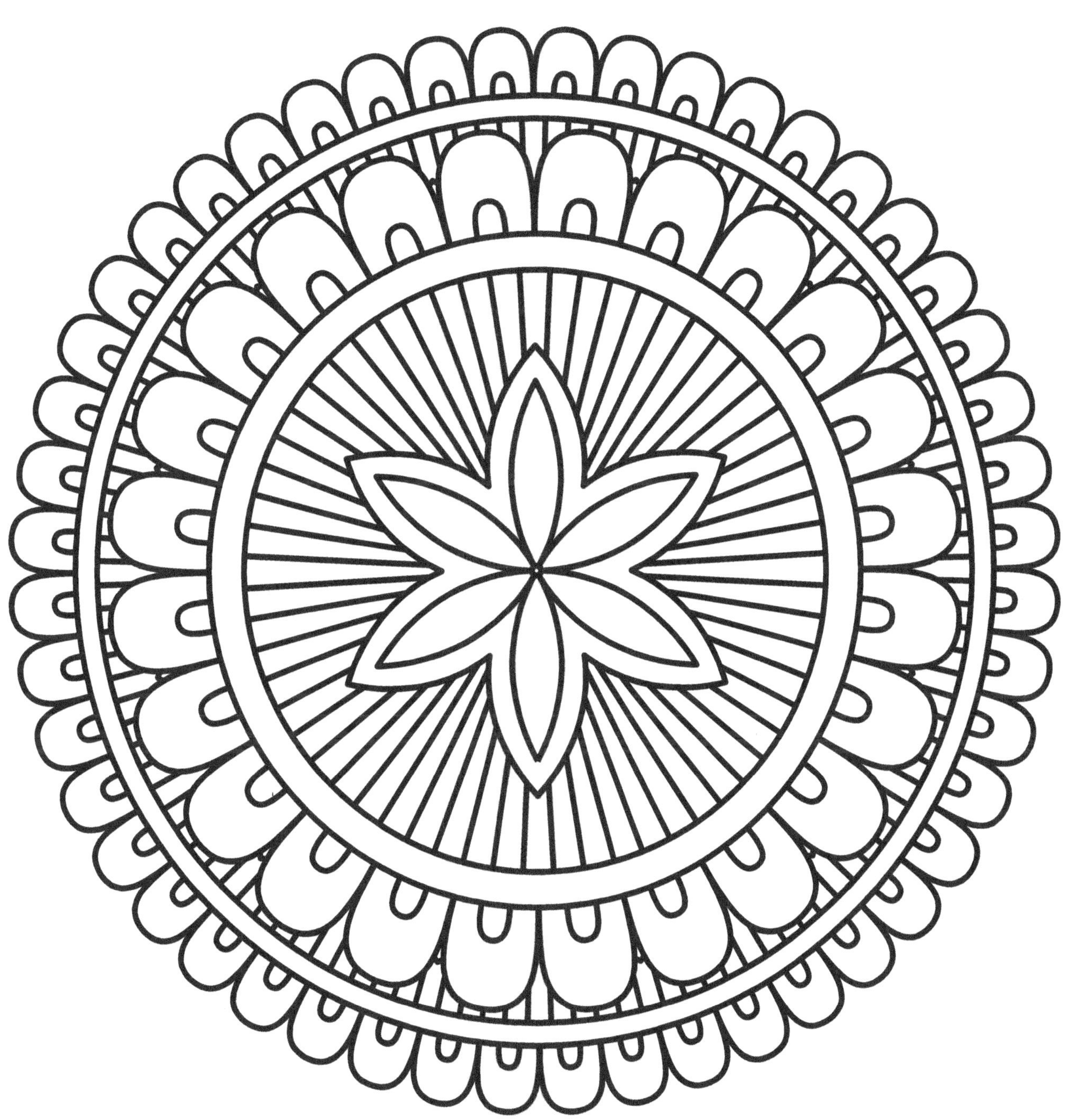

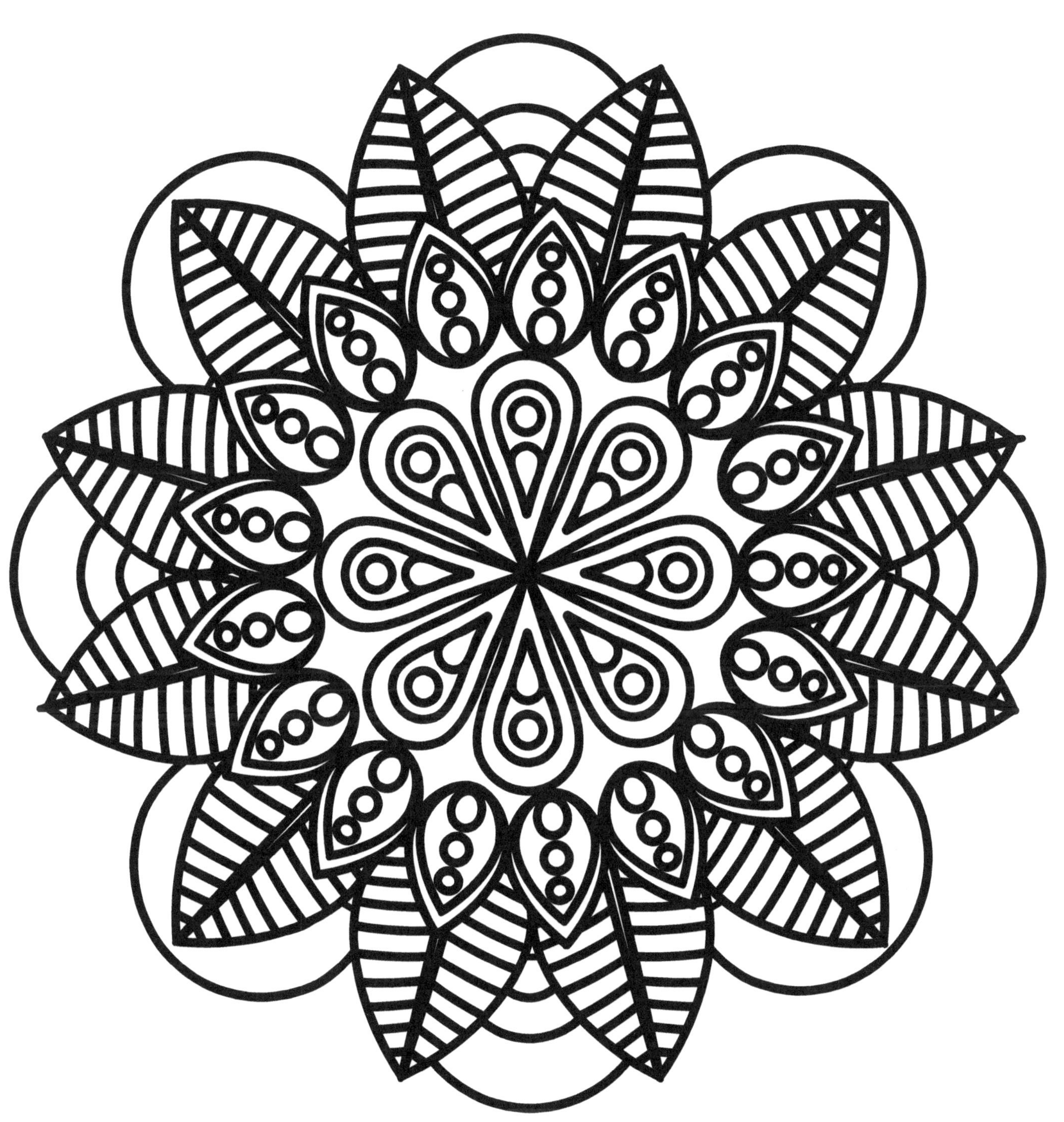

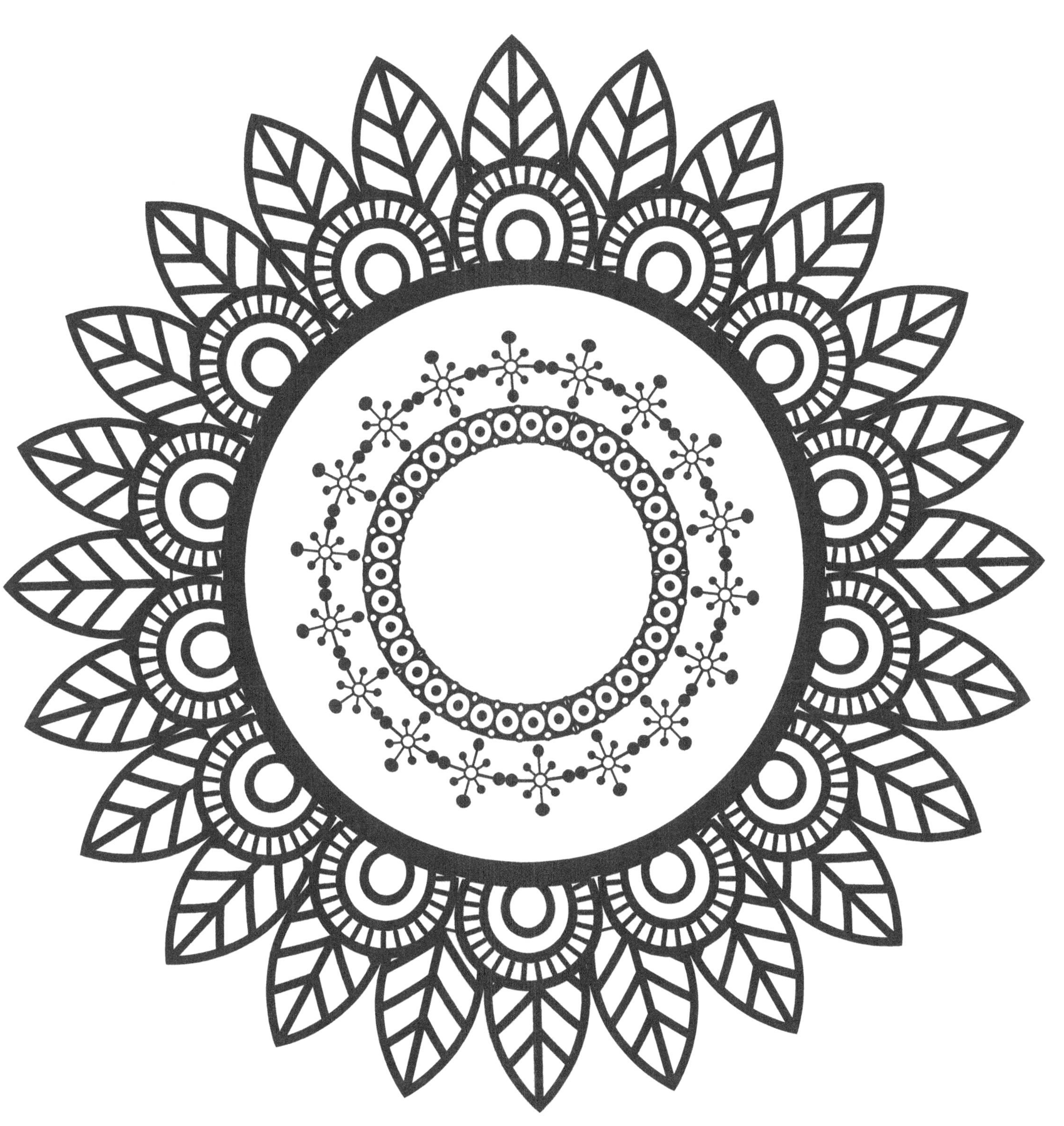

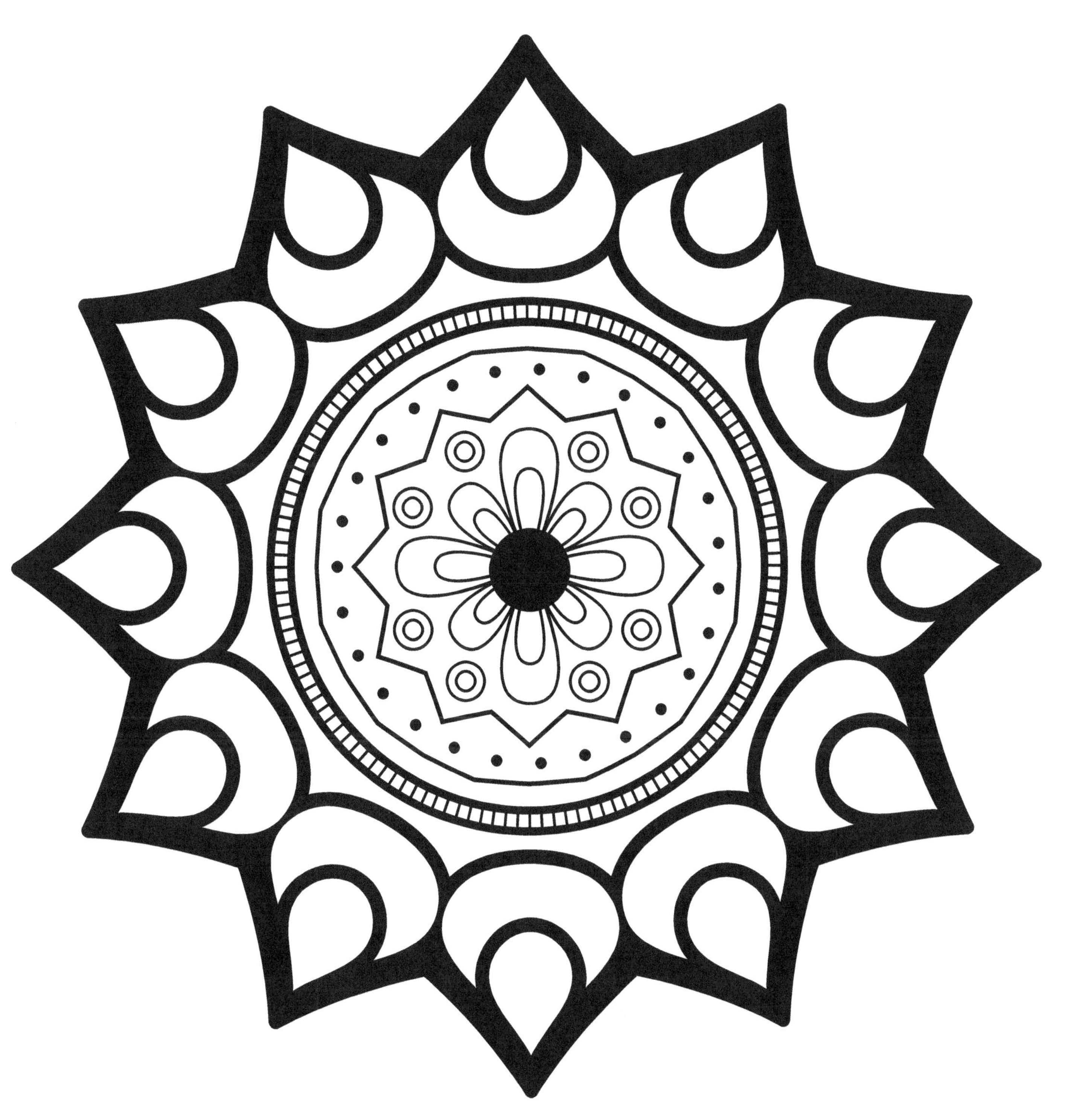

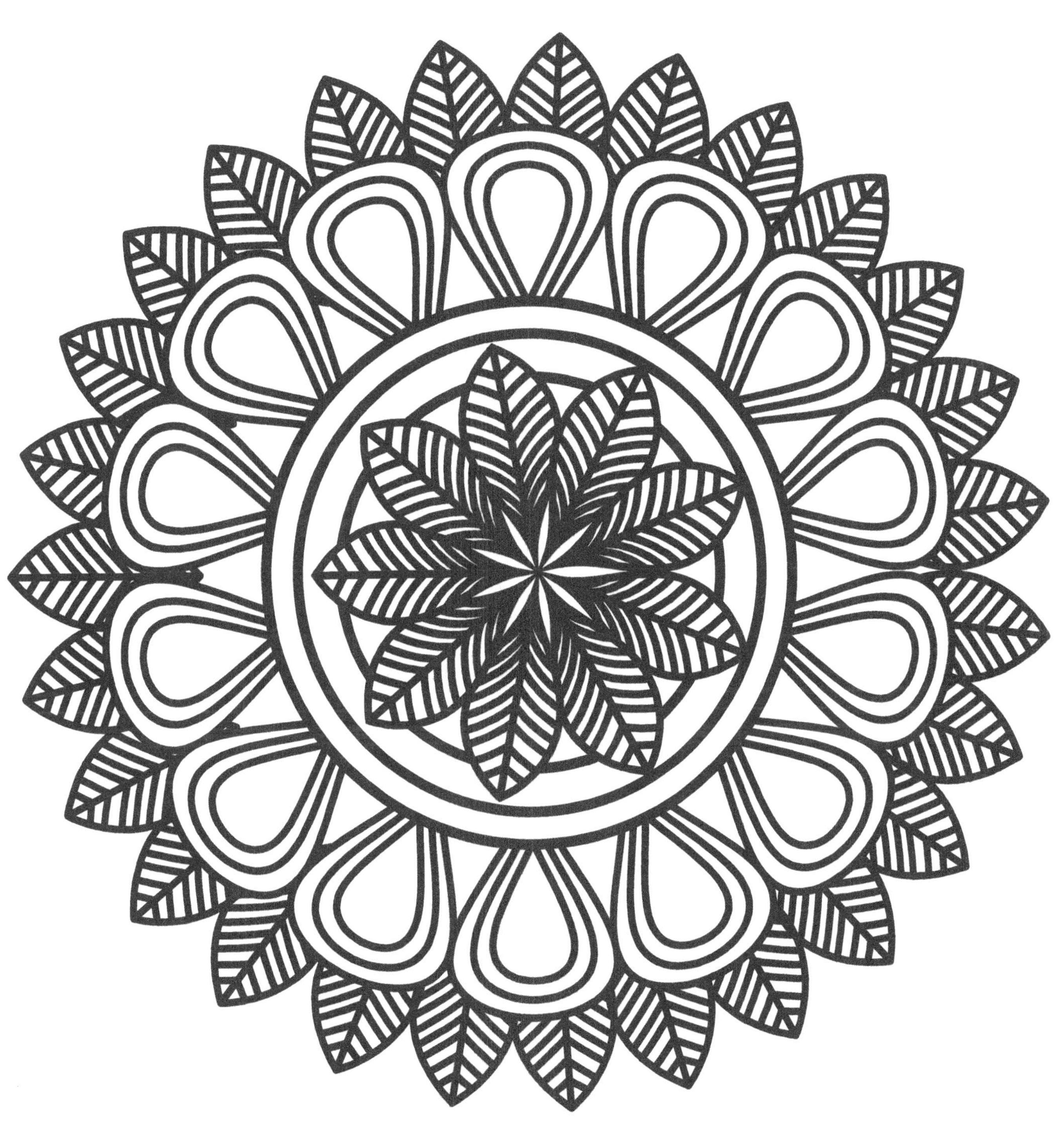

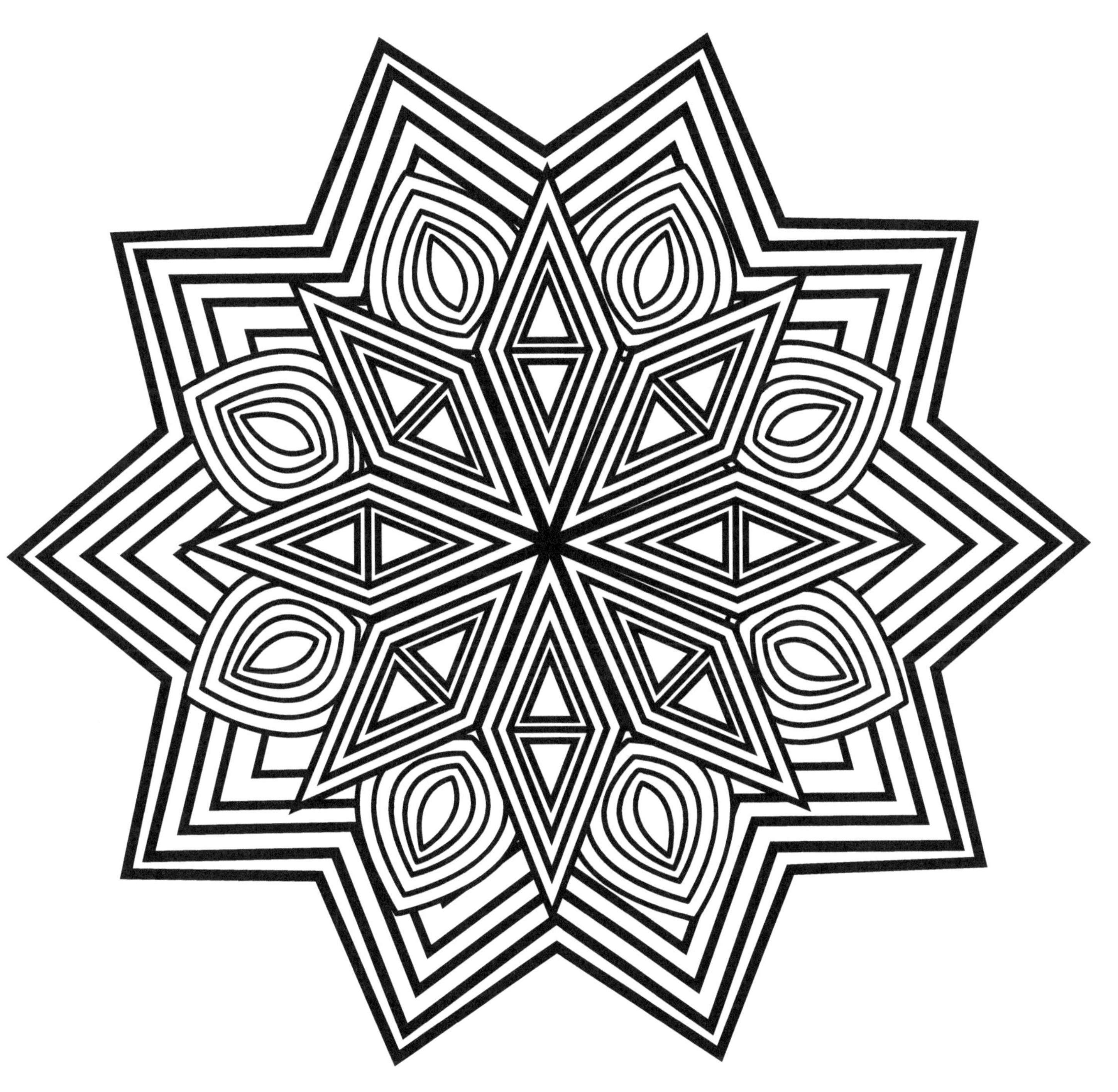